How to Be Together on Sunday Morning

HOW · TO · FAMILY
SERIES

How to Be
Together
on
Sunday
Morning

Jane L. Fryar

CPH™
SAINT LOUIS

How to Family Series

How to Be a Great First-Time Father
How to Be Together on Sunday Morning
How to Enjoy a Healthy Family
(Even in Stressful Times)

Unless otherwise noted, Scripture quotations are taken from THE HOLY BIBLE, NEW INTERNATIONAL VERSION®. Copyright © 1973, 1978, 1984 by the International Bible Society. Used by permission of Zondervan Publishing House. All rights reserved.

The "NIV" and "New International Version" trademarks are registered in the United States Patent and Trademark Office by the International Bible Society. Use of either trademark requires the permission of the International Bible Society.

Copyright © 1995 Concordia Publishing House
3558 South Jefferson Avenue, St. Louis, MO 63118-3968
Manufactured in the United States of America

Library of Congress Cataloging-in-Publication Data

Fryar, Jane, 1950–
    How to be together on Sunday / Jane Fryar.
        p.   cm.   —(How to family series)
    ISBN 0-570-04690-4
    1. Family—Religious life. 2. Christian life.
  I. Title. II. Series.
  BV4526.2.F76 1995
  248.4—dc20   94-45402

1 2 3 4 5 6 7 8 9 10   04 03 02 01 00 99 98 97 96 95

CONTENTS

1

WHAT AM I
DOING HERE?

A song popular in the 1960s told the story of a young draftee who rode with General Custer into the battle of the Little Bighorn. The lyrics betray the soldier's dread at the approaching battle. At the same time, they poke fun at his fears.

Toward the end of the song, shortly after the battle is joined, we hear the hapless soldier mutter to himself, "What am I doing here?" No one answers his question.

Questions That Count

Maybe you've asked that question yourself. Maybe you've asked it about your marriage, about your family. Perhaps as you ask it now you feel frustrated or angry, betrayed or confused, condemned or rejected. Perhaps like the draftee in General Custer's army, you feel alone and afraid. What am I doing here? in this marriage? in this family?

Sometimes, a Christian who marries a non-Christian thinks the spiritual differences between them won't matter that much. Sometimes, Christians simply assume that their marriage partner shares their faith because they've seen their potential partner attend church on a fairly regular basis. Sometimes, two people share about the same level of spiritual interest, belief, and commitment on their wedding day, but at a later date, one of them begins to grow in the faith by leaps and bounds, leaving the other behind.

No matter how spiritual differences enter a marriage relationship, they always matter. A lot. They often hurt. A lot. Spiritual differences can complicate any relationship. Because God has designed the marriage relationship as one of life's most intimate, spiritual differences complicate marriage relationships more than any other human relationship.

David and Debbie

David grew up in a Christian home near Tulsa. His parents took him to church and sent him to Sunday school on a fairly regular basis. He dated Debbie, a friend he had met at a church junior high youth event, throughout their high school years. During David's last year in engineering school, they were married.

Even though the two had not talked much about spiritual issues before their marriage, David assumed he and Debbie would attend church together after the wedding. And they did, for a month or so. But before long, Debbie began missing worship services once or twice a month. Since both of them worked hard all week, she said it would feel good to be able to sleep in once in a while.

A month or two later, Debbie got pregnant. Morning sickness made staying in bed on Sunday morning even easier. By the time the baby came, Debbie had stopped making excuses. She had also stopped making any effort to be involved at church at all.

David feels bewildered and estranged. "What are we doing here?" he wonders. "And what should—or can—I do now?"

Craig and Cynthia

Both Craig and Cynthia grew up in families where alcohol was abused. Cynthia's father, a professional church worker, left the ministry when his congregation confronted him and asked him to enter counseling. He refused, moved his family to another state, and took a job as an insurance salesman. Cynthia saw less and less of him after that, as he spent more and more of his time on the road, covering what eventually became a very large, lucrative territory.

Cynthia's mom insisted that she and her brother attend church until eighth grade. Then she let Cynthia make up her own mind. Cynthia dropped out.

Craig's dad was never guilty of the kind of benign neglect Cynthia suffered. Craig remembers nightly shouting matches that ended in physical abuse two or three times each week, every week, during Craig's growing-up years.

Craig doesn't know it, but lodged deep in his heart is the fear that his heavenly Father has as little regard for him as did his earthly father. Craig does know, though, that he's angry at God. He freely admits that fact. He brandishes it like a shield anytime anyone invites him to do anything remotely religious. The last time he stepped inside a church was back in second grade when a neighborhood friend invited him to vacation Bible school.

Neither Craig nor Cynthia thought of their marriage as a Christian one on their wedding day. But about a year ago, Cynthia went back to church "for the children." After a few weeks had passed, the Holy Spirit had set Cynthia's heart ablaze with love for the Lord Jesus and with excitement about His love for her.

In the months since then, Cynthia has joined two Bible study groups and a prayer group. She sings in the senior choir and has started a campaign to introduce handbells into the congregation's worship services. Every time the doors of the church open, it seems that Cynthia is there.

Craig, meanwhile, finds himself confused and

even a bit frightened. He wonders whether Cynthia may have gotten mixed up with a cult of some kind. He wonders what he'll do "if she gets any more fanatic." Most of all, he wonders how he can compete with God for first place in his wife's heart.

Larry and Lucy

Lucy knew Larry came from a non-Christian background. She knew he didn't believe much—not in heaven or hell, not in angels or miracles, not in sin or forgiveness, not even in God Himself.

Still, they seemed so perfect for each other. Everyone told them that. They even looked like they belonged together. Or so their friends said.

Lucy's parents weren't so sure. Divorced themselves a decade earlier, both Dad and Mom tried to get Lucy to change her mind. "Talk it over now," Lucy's mom urged. "Get it straight from the beginning. How will he feel if you want to pray or read the Bible? Will he come to church with you—or let you go alone? What happens when the kids come along? Will he help you get them to Sunday school? Talk to him, Lucy!"

But Lucy was afraid. Afraid that if she spoke up, Larry would think she was having second thoughts. Afraid he'd back off. Afraid she'd lose him. So she said nothing.

"Once we settle down he'll change," Lucy

thought. "We love each other. It will all work out." The pain in her heart shines through her eyes as she says, "I was wrong. I had no idea how wrong, until the children came along."

Lucy expends a mountain of effort each week as she tries to meet her children's need for spiritual nurture as well as their physical and emotional needs. Working full-time as a paramedic for a local ambulance service, Lucy often finds herself out of energy before she's out of tasks. She wishes she could pull off family devotions, but some weeks it's all she can manage to get the kids ready for Sunday school while Larry reads the Sunday paper in his pajamas.

Robert and Rachael

Robert met Rachael in graduate school. He was studying to be a school counselor, she a physician. Robert attended a Christian elementary school and a Christian high school. His Savior had always been important to him. So had his church.

Rachael's parents were Jewish and she thought of herself as Jewish too. But while her parents attended temple regularly, Rachael had not practiced Judaism since her teen years.

Rachael promised Robert she would support him in raising their children in the Christian faith, and she kept that promise during their children's early years. But now that their two boys have grown a bit older, Rachael has begun to invite them along as she makes hospital rounds each Sunday morning.

The boys like nothing better than going to work with Mom. So now Robert finds himself negotiating with his sons, neither yet 10 years old, about the one thing that matters most to him in the world. No matter how hard Robert tries to explain his feelings, Rachael just doesn't seem to understand his concern.

Put Away the Band-Aids

You may see a mirror image of yourself and your marriage reflected in one of the scenarios you just read. Or your situation may differ markedly. Either way, anyone who presumes to propose a simple answer to dilemmas like these, to conflicts like these, to pain like this hasn't paid attention to the complexities of real life. If simple answers would work, you would have used them. And you wouldn't have waited until now to do it.

It's easy to flip a gunshot victim a Band-Aid. It's easy to shout, "Trust God," to a drowning victim. It's easy to intone, "It will all work out," to a friend who has just been fired. Easy, but ineffective. Easy, but callous. Even cruel.

The pages that follow will not propose easy answers. I won't presume to unknot every complication you face. I don't intend to prescribe "four simple steps to peace at home." Or eight steps. Or even 124 steps. There just are no easy answers, no quick fixes.

On the other hand, your Lord does want to offer you help and support—support that comes directly from His heart, help that comes directly from His throne. Many of His people have learned to use His Word and His power to cope with situations as painful and complex as yours. You can, by His grace, grow in that ability too.

Where Are You Coming From?

That's a fair question to ask, since you as reader must commit time and effort to understanding and applying the concepts presented in the chapters that follow. And especially since, if you decide to do that, the concepts may very well change your marriage, your relationships with those closest to you—your children, your other relatives, and perhaps your friends. The concepts that follow may even change your relationship with your Lord Jesus.

That's why I've taken time to detail—up front— the six foundational assumptions that underlie this book.

Principle 1—You are important to God.

So important that for the joy of living with you forever, our heavenly Father sent His Son, Jesus, to live and die for you. You are of infinite worth because God paid an infinite price for you. He paid an infinite price *for you*!

As the sun hung black against an inky sky for hours on the Friday we Christians call good, God turned His back on His own Son's suffering. He abandoned Jesus to the horrors of hell because He did not ever want to abandon you in your sins.

Because of what Christ did, God now promises never, ever to abandon you. No sin ... no worry ... no lapse of judgment ... no doubt ... no defection ... no anger ... no need ... no disappointment—nothing, absolutely nothing can stop your Father's love for you.

That same Lord, your Lord, is active in your life every day. Your Lord thinks about you every minute. He continually plans ways to bring good things into your life. He dotes on you; He can't help Himself. It's just the way He is—He *is* love! He is totally and eternally committed to your welfare, and you can't dissuade Him from that commitment, not even if you decide to try.

Principle 2—*Your marriage partner is important to God too.*

Your wife is not the enemy. Your husband is not the adversary. God loves your spouse every bit as much as He loves you. Jesus died with both of you in His mind, in His heart.

In fact, God loves your partner more than you

do. God loves each of you more deeply than you can ever imagine loving one another. He's even more committed to you than you are to each other.

The Holy Spirit longs to draw both of you closer and closer to your God. Just as you can't do anything to get God to stop loving you, neither can your marriage partner stop God's love, God's commitment to him or her.

If the ultimate tragedy occurs, if your spouse persists in rejecting God's love, consistently refuses God's offer of forgiveness and adoption into His family, if your spouse never gives in and lets God give the gift of eternal life He so wants to give, the Father's heart will grieve that tragedy. The Father's heart will ache with that loss, that rejection. That's how committed our Lord is to His human creatures, to all His human creatures. (See, for instance, Rom. 10:21 and Hos. 11:2–8.) Each of us—your spouse too—is that important to God.

Principle 3—*You and your family matter to the family of God.*

The Lone Ranger may have made a great television folk hero. But lone-ranger faith won't make it across the deserts of life's real challenges. It won't survive the storms of life.

You may feel that no one in the church cares about you. You may even have accumulated a mountain of evidence to prove it. You may feel that no one in the church needs you. You may have accumulated a mountain of evidence to prove your own inability to help (or even to care about) your Christian brothers and sisters.

Regardless of how you feel, though, the fact remains that you and the members of your earthly family are important to the rest of us in God's family. You need support and help from us. We need your insights, your help, your support too.

You cannot go it alone. Neither can we. None of us dare try.

Principle 4—God's truth, spoken in love, can help.

Our culture has all but abandoned the idea of absolute truth. Instead, we find ourselves bombarded with self-styled experts who chant such helpful phrases as:

"It all depends ..."

"I feel that ..."

"In this case I think that ..."

"If it works for you ..."

Our culture has corrupted our understanding of specific and critical truths, truths God has given us—not to hurt us or to deny us independence or pleasure but rather to help us through the knotty situations of life. Sometimes we're not even aware of how distorted our picture of reality is.

That's why we must align our opinions with the truths God has given us in His book, the Holy Scriptures. When someone decides, "I know what the Bible says, but I think it's best for me to do something else instead," hope for help or peace in that area of that person's life evaporates.

Nowhere have God's principles been more corrupted than in our culture's concepts of marriage and family. The constant barrage of relativistic advice given by well-meaning media experts, our neighbors, and friends will leave us lost in a fog of confusion. It can even keep us from hearing what the Scriptures say when we read God's will in black and white. That's why we must continually renew our minds, as the Bible says, in the truths our Lord wants us to know.

But truth—even God's truth—spoken lovelessly or to condemn will not help anyone. Too often, some in the church lecture and sermonize, sermonize and lecture without loving, without caring much about the needs and the pain of those to whom they speak. Truth spoken without love, spoken without Christ-like compassion, is bankrupt. It is powerless. It drives people away from the Savior who wants to receive and comfort them.

We need to hear God's truth from one another. Sometimes we may swallow hard first, but we need to accept and act on the truth that is God's truth. We also need to speak God's truth to one another in the same authentic, self-giving love Jesus Himself would show if He visibly appeared to join our conversation.

Principle 5—Realism will help; magical thinking will not.

People in difficult circumstances often minimize their own plight. "It isn't so bad," they tell themselves. "We'll get along okay." One big problem with minimizing lies in the fact that people often deal with the problems they minimize by ignoring them.

- If David refuses to ask how Debbie feels about the possibility of him teaching a Bible study at the Smith's house each Wednesday night, he loses an important opportunity to understand and meet Debbie's emotional needs and, perhaps, her spiritual ones too. Telling himself, "It's no big deal; of course, she'll understand," and then not finding out whether it's a big deal to her or not is unloving to her and disrespectful of their relationship.

- If Cynthia ignores Craig's sarcastic comments about her new-found Christian friends, she allows another brick to fall into place in the wall that is slowly but surely being erected between them. By minimizing her hurt, by telling herself,

"He didn't mean anything by it," Cynthia also may rob herself of the chance to understand and root out seeds of jealousy and fear that have begun to sprout in Craig's heart.

If we have a problem—any problem—we must admit it exists and that it matters to us. Only then will we take steps to resolve it. Until then it will remain unsolved and unsolvable.

Once we acknowledge our need, it's essential that we give up hoping in magical solutions. Instead, we must ask God for the wisdom to know and the courage to do whatever He holds us responsible for doing in the situation. Finally, having done what we can do, we must leave the results to Him.

There is no tooth fairy. No one—not even God Himself—will come along your path in life, touch your forehead with a magic wand, and with a POOF make all your family conflicts disappear. No one—not even God Himself—will flip a switch in your spouse's heart, thereby turning your partner, robot-like, into a believer. Sad to say, well-meaning Christian counselors sometimes make promises like these for God, promises that He has never made.

Perhaps someone has already laid a list of magical "if onlys" on you:

If only you submit to your husband completely enough ...

If only you shower your wife with enough affection ...

If only you pray long enough and hard enough for your children ...

Then your husband or wife or children will
... become believers.
... want to come to church.
... participate in family devotions.
... be polite to the pastor next time he calls.
... pray with you every day.

God has made many specific, wonderful promises to us and He keeps them all. We, however, need to understand exactly what He has promised to do for us and, perhaps just as importantly, what He has not. Only then can we think realistically, not magically. Only then can we think and act in godly hope. Only then can we make sound decisions in our relationships and know—on the strength of God's Word—that He will back us up, that He will back us all the way.

Principle 6—Change happens only as God works in willing hearts.

We're all in process. Someday all of God's children will be fully like the Lord Jesus, our big brother. Until then, we will sometimes make mistakes. We will hurt others—even those we love the most. We will act thoughtlessly and selfishly. We will need our

Lord's forgiveness. With that forgiveness always comes the power to change, to grow, to continue down the road toward increasing holiness. We cannot change ourselves. If change is to happen, we must ask our Lord Himself to work it in us.

Knowing that we cannot change even ourselves, we can see that it's the height of folly to try to change anyone else. Husband, you can't convert your wife. Wife, you won't transform your husband. Change—especially spiritual change—is the Holy Spirit's work. If you insist on trying to do His job, you will wear yourself out. Chances are good that you'll irritate your spouse to no end. Chances are also good that you'll harden him or her in the very attitudes and behaviors that you hate.

Each of us has enough need for change inside our own hearts and minds. We don't need to poke our noses into the hearts and minds of others. Ask God for the grace you need to concentrate on you. Ask God to help you want the changes He wants to make in you. Ask God to make those changes. Then ask Him for peace as you leave change in others to Him.

Before You Go On

1. If someone would write a scenario (like the ones that began this chapter) about your spiritual heritage and your current marriage rela-

tionship, what might it include?

2. What, for you, are the two or three most difficult spiritual problems you face in your marriage relationship today? What makes these particular issues so important for you?

3. Reread the six principles that ended this chapter.

   a. With which do you agree?

   b. Which do you question? Why?

   c. From your perspective, why is each important to a discussion of this particular topic?

WHAT ABOUT ME?

Spiritual loneliness. Have you ever experienced it? Probably so. Many circumstances can foster it. Marriage to someone who does not share a commitment to Jesus is one of them. Many times, the victims of spiritual loneliness are oblivious to what's happening to them. The numbness masks the pain while the disease grows worse.

What is spiritual loneliness? We might define it informally as the sadness (leading ultimately to despair) that grows in a believer's heart when he or she is isolated from direct, meaningful, Word-filled contact with other Christians.

God's children want to be encouraged and to encourage one another in His truth. We want to worship Him and pray together. We want to participate in the family meal, the Lord's Supper. The Holy Spirit stimulates this kind of hunger and thirst in our hearts. When we do not access opportunities to quench that spiritual thirst, we grow heart-sick. Our souls begin to shrivel. Sometimes they callous over.

We have begun the slow march down the road toward spiritual death.

Can God sustain His children in isolation from other believers? Of course. Believers have endured years of solitary confinement under totalitarian governments intent on destroying their Christian faith. Individual missionaries have labored on alone after their fellow workers died from disease or at the hands of those to whom they ministered.

These exceptions, however, do not disprove the general rule. God intends that His people live in spiritual community. He intends for *all* of His people to live in spiritual community. When we find ourselves isolated—either physically or emotionally—from other believers, the isolation soon begins to take its toll on our relationship with our Lord.

While the term itself does not appear in the Scriptures, the concept recurs there. King David surely understood it firsthand. Tip-toe into his throne room. Stand quietly for a moment in a corner and eavesdrop on a few of his prayers:

> *Turn to me and be gracious to me, [LORD,] for I am lonely and afflicted.* (Ps. 25:16)

> *My friends and companions avoid me because of my wounds; my neighbors stay far away. ... I am about to fall, and my pain is ever with me. I*

confess my iniquity; I am troubled by my sin. ...
O LORD, *do not forsake me; be not far from me,*
O my God. (Ps. 38:11, 17–18, 21)

[My enemies] say, "God has forsaken him; pur-
sue him and seize him, for no one will rescue
him." (Ps. 71:11)

David's words strike several chords. We hear his
conscience playing guilt's melody in a minor key. We
hear his words toll the death knell of his dreams. But
we also hear the haunting strains of isolation, the pain
felt by one of God's children who faces life's problems alone—without God and without support from
other believers.

Have you ever felt like that? Spiritually alone
like that?

Maybe you wouldn't paste that label on your
experience. Maybe you've chalked up your discomfort to job stress or to last night's disagreement (a.k.a.
argument) with your spouse or to the headache you
had when you got up this morning. But regardless of
the dodging and denying we do, spiritual loneliness
is real.

Check Yourself Out

The informal survey below will help you put
your finger on areas of your spiritual life in which
you feel alone. Fill it out before you move on.

Never Sometimes Often

_____ _____ _____ 1. I feel awkward sitting in church by myself; sometimes I'm tempted to skip worship so I don't have to go alone.

_____ _____ _____ 2. I wish I had someone to talk to about the Lord and what He's doing in my life.

_____ _____ _____ 3. I wish I had someone to pray with on a regular basis.

_____ _____ _____ 4. I tell myself that if I can be a good enough wife/husband, my spouse will eventually come to faith in Jesus.

_____ _____ _____ 5. I feel I shouldn't be weak in my faith or express worries and doubts because it would be a bad witness to my spouse (family).

_____ _____ _____ 6. I feel pressure from inside myself or from other people to get my spouse to come to faith.

_____ _____ _____ 7. I feel pressure from my my spouse to take my relationship with Jesus less seriously.

_____ _____ _____ 8. I struggle with feelings of guilt or shame for not living up to God's standards for my life.

_____ _____ _____ 9. I wish that I had someone to help me figure out what God might want me to do when I face important decisions.

_____ _____ _____ 10. (if applicable) I worry about the spiritual well-being of my children, and I feel I bear almost all the responsibility for it.

To score this quiz, give yourself 2 points for every *often* you checked, 1 point for every *sometimes*, and 0 points for every *never*. Then add up your total points.

If you scored 0–3 points, you can thank God for putting Christian brothers and sisters in your life who support and encourage you in your walk with Him.

If you scored 4–6 points, you probably could use more support from other believers, and you need to pray and think about ways to find it.

If you scored more than 6 points, you definitely need to ask the Lord Jesus for help with the spiritual isolation you're experiencing. You may feel spiritually lonely. You may be aware of the erosion taking place in your relationship with the Lord. Or you may have deadened yourself to the loneliness somehow. Nevertheless, you're living with a ticking spiritual time bomb buried in your heart. It's time to call out the bomb squad. Now.

The Deepest Part of You

Is spiritual isolation all that dangerous? Yes. We shrivel up and die when we try to live apart from relationship with other members of God's family. We also shrivel up and die when we live in the family as though the others there were our third or fourth cousins rather than our brothers and sisters. You see, our Father created us for relationship—for intimate relationship—with Himself and with each other.

A decade or so ago, slogans like these became popular:

Joining a church will make you a Christian when entering a garage makes you a car.

Going to church will make you a Christian when walking into a barn makes you a horse.

In one sense, of course, these statements are exactly right. We're not Christians because we belong to XYZ denomination. We're not Christians because we've joined St. Monolith Church. We're Christians because God has joined us to Himself in Christ by His grace through faith in what He did for us on the cross.

Yet our relationship with Jesus is not our only relationship in the family of God. The Holy Spirit forged other essential relationships for us when He brought us into His family. Those of us who belong to Jesus Christ also belong to one another. If Jesus is your brother and He's my brother, then I'm your sister too. Like it or not. And our relationship is an eternal one.

It's a good thing. Because I need you. You need me. Outside our need for Jesus, our need for relationship with Christian brothers and sisters is our deepest need. We need to hear the encouragement of God's Word from one another. We need to draw strength and support from one another during times of trial and temptation. We need one another's prayers.

From time to time, we also need other believers to point out our sin and its dangers. We need other believers around us who will warn us if we begin to drift away from our moorings. All believers need this kind of help from one another. That's why our Lord urges, pleads, and, yes, commands us to take an active role in a local congregation, to find ourselves involved with His family regularly, and to interact on more than a surface level.

Especially if you do not receive encouragement from God's Word at home, especially if you do not receive prayer support at home, you need to seek it out from your church. You need to ask the Lord Jesus for the wisdom and courage to take the initiative. Don't wait for someone from your congregation to come to you:

- Worship with other believers regularly—even if doing that alone feels awkward or out of place at first. Ask the Holy Spirit for the grace to avoid being lulled into complacency. Remember what the Scripture says:

  Let us not give up meeting together, as some are

in the habit of doing, but let us encourage one another—and all the more as you see the Day approaching. (Heb. 10:25)

- Come to the Lord's Table every chance you get. Ask the Holy Spirit to help you better understand and draw strength from the unity He creates in His family as we share Jesus' body and blood there.

- Talk with your pastor about opportunities for group Bible study during the week in addition to Sunday morning. Then ask the Holy Spirit to help you plug into a group of believers who will encourage you and whom you can encourage.

- Find someone willing to be your prayer partner. Ask God's Spirit to lead you to someone of the same gender who is supportive of you and of your situation. Then look for someone open enough to listen to your prayer needs and to share his or her own. Both of you need to agree to keep the information you discuss confidential. And you need to agree to ask God to keep your hearts sensitive so that "sharing prayer needs" won't become an excuse for gossip.

- Ask the Holy Spirit to keep you keenly aware of your spiritual thirst. Then quench that thirst as you read the Scriptures each day. Look for opportunities to talk about what God is showing you in His Word with other believers—your new prayer partner, for instance.

Don't discount these suggestions just because most of them sound familiar. Most times, those whose faith ends up in splinters on the rocks haven't gone off course by ignoring some obscure navigational technique. Most times, they have simply fallen asleep at the rudder.

Don't open yourself up to that possibility. Don't put yourself in a position in which you're likely to drift away from the Lord and from His family. In short, don't try to live in your family as if you had no church home.

Committees or Committed?

Aware of the dangers of drifting away, some believers throw themselves into every activity their congregation offers. Remember David and Debbie from chapter 1?

Some months after Debbie stopped showing interest in spiritual matters, David started staying after the weekly worship service to attend Bible class. The class leader, a retired pastor, took a personal interest in David.

One Sunday after class, the pastor stopped David and invited him to join the congregation's social ministry group the following Wednesday evening. David did. Soon after, someone from the church called and asked David to serve as assistant Sunday school superintendent.

Six months later, David found himself at the church building three or four nights each week. Debbie, home-bound most days with a toddler, grew colder and seemingly more resentful of David's time away from home. But she didn't bring the topic up for discussion, and David couldn't seem to muster the courage he needed to broach the subject.

Besides, David had begun to feel more fulfilled, more content with his life and its direction than ever before. His friends at church kept on applauding his commitment and assuring him how much they needed him. How could he disappoint his congregation by backing out of any of those commitments now—even if that's what Debbie might want him to do?

It can happen so subtly. Few congregations have all the volunteer workers they need or could use. Well-meaning congregational leaders scout potential recruits like commuters looking for a chance to grab the last vacant seat on the bus. Just as individual families can behave dysfunctionally, so can church families. Rather than canceling or postponing programs we can't staff, we often simply look until we find warm bodies to throw into the breach.

When that happens, programs suffer. The congregation suffers. The program leaders and congregational leaders suffer. Families suffer. And marriages suffer.

Debbie probably sees the situation more clearly than David. While we can't diagnose David's congregation as dysfunctional based on the information contained in the scenario above, the evidence certainly seems to point in that direction.

Debbie, no doubt, is angry—at David, at the church, and probably at God too. Her heart has, no doubt, hardened a bit further as she's lived through the events of the past year. She cannot legitimately blame her increasing bitterness on David, on the church, or on God. She has chosen bitterness rather than risk confronting David. But Debbie does have a legitimate complaint at David's neglect of her and of their son.

David, on the other hand, almost certainly fails to comprehend the process at work in his own heart. He has allowed church activities to become a substitute for the spiritual intimacy he needs but doesn't get from Debbie. Without intending to do so, he's actually diminishing the chances that he will ever be able to share the deepest part of himself—his relationship with Christ—with his wife.

How could David have avoided this pitfall? How can he crawl out of it now? No one can tell David how much church-centered activity is enough. Are three committees and two Bible classes too much? Is Sunday morning worship and Tuesday evening prayer group enough? It's an individual decision, one each of us must make prayerfully and after careful thought.

At the heart of this decision-making process lies the question, "What would Jesus have me do?" That question takes into account these key factors:

- Your need for encouragement and support from your brothers and sisters in the faith.
- Your family's need for your presence, help, godly example, and love.
- Your physical and emotional energy.
- The needs of your congregation.
- The interests you have; the talents, gifts, and abilities God has given you; and the ways your gifts match the needs of your congregation.

Think through ways to balance all these factors as you budget your time. Pray through them as you allocate your energy. In short, don't live in the church as if you had no family.

When the Jury Returns a Guilty Verdict

Of course, none of us balances our time in a God-pleasing way with perfection. Spiritual loneliness sprouts like a garden-variety weed in the fertile soil of guilt. And failures in time management aren't the only failures that pull us down. As you began this chapter, you read the psalmist's guilty plea:

*I confess my iniquity; I am troubled by my sin.
... O LORD, do not forsake me; be not far from
me, O my God.* (Ps. 38:18, 21)

Have you ever felt that way? Has it ever seemed
that God was far away and that He was about to
leave you alone without sending you a forwarding
address? If so, you're in good company. Remember
Lucy and Larry from chapter 1?

*For the first five years of their marriage, Lucy felt
guilty for marrying Larry in the first place. Every Sunday
as she dressed the children for church, she heard her mother's warnings ringing in her ears. Why had she ignored
them all? Why hadn't she realized how important Jesus
was to her and how important it would be that her family
worshiped Him together?*

*As time went on, the focus of Lucy's guilt shifted. A
Christian friend directed her to the advice of St. Peter:*

Wives, in the same way be submissive to your
husbands so that, if any of them do not believe
the word, they may be won over without words
by the behavior of their wives, when they see the
purity and reverence of your lives. (1 Peter
3:1–2)

*As Lucy thought about that Scripture, she became
convinced that if she could set a godly-enough example,
Larry was bound to come to faith. So Lucy worked hard at*

becoming just what Larry wanted her to be, to do just what Larry wanted her to do.

One of the paramedics with whom she worked began calling her "Super Spouse." Still, Larry showed little interest in the Lord Jesus.

Everything came to a head one day as Lucy sat in her pastor's study wiping her eyes with a sodden tissue. "I hate it!" she sobbed. "I'm so tired of trying to be the perfect Christian wife. I always have to be strong. I can't ever feel down or doubtful or worried. I can't ever be weak. When I do, Larry just looks at me and shakes his head. 'What good does that faith of yours do you, Lucy?' he'll ask. I want to scream at him. Sometimes I do. And then I feel even more guilty. What's wrong with me anyway, Pastor?"

What's wrong with Lucy? Satan has taken a pinch of the truth, mixed it thoroughly with a few gallons of his lies, and popped it into the ovens of hell to create a huge casserole of guilt. Now he's force-feeding it to her. Lucy needs to hear some truth:

- Jesus Christ is the only perfect child of God ever to have walked around on this earth. He alone never sinned. In fact, He came to earth precisely because the rest of us *do* sin. We can rely on Him to forgive and accept us when we fail to take our relationship with Him seriously enough and when we fail to live lives of perfect trust, perfect witness.

- The Holy Spirit leads people to faith and strengthens them in that faith. We pray for the unsaved and for those weak in their faith. We witness to them. But we cannot manipulate or argue or shame someone else into a relationship with Jesus. We can—and we must—turn over to God the responsibility for the spiritual lives of those we love.

- All of us are human. By definition, humans are creatures with limitations. We have limited time, abilities, energy.

- Limits are not sinful; failure to recognize our limitations can be.

- We have the freedom, under God, to be weak— even weak in faith. As our brother Paul pointed out so many centuries ago, it's only when we are weak that we can be truly strong. Only when we admit our weakness, our desperate need for God's strength and for relying on Him instead of on ourselves, only then can His grace work fully in our lives. He put it this way:

[The Lord] said to me, "My grace is sufficient for you, for My power is made perfect in weakness."

Therefore I will boast all the more gladly about my weaknesses, so that Christ's power may rest on me. That is why, for Christ's sake, I delight in

weaknesses. ... For when I am weak, then I am
strong. (2 Cor. 12:9–10)

Does all this mean that Lucy can excuse herself for the sin in her life? Of course not. Nor would she, as God's daughter, want to do that. Lucy, like the rest of us, needs to confess her sins and receive God's thorough forgiveness and cleansing.

What it does mean, though, is that Lucy needs to reexamine the standards she has set for herself. Peter's advice to wives with unbelieving spouses, for example, was meant to unburden people like Lucy— not to lay new burdens on them. Read his words in context once more (or maybe even twice!):

Wives, in the same way be submissive to your
husbands so that, if any of them do not believe
the word, they may be won over without words
by the behavior of their wives, when they see the
purity and reverence of your lives.

Your beauty should not come from outward
adornment, such as braided hair and the wearing
of gold jewelry and fine clothes. Instead, it
should be that of your inner self, the unfading
beauty of a gentle and quiet spirit, which is of
great worth in God's sight.

For this is the way the holy women of the past

who put their hope in God used to make them-
selves beautiful. They were submissive to their
own husbands, like Sarah, who obeyed Abraham
and called him her master. You are her daughters
if you do what is right and do not give way to
fear. (1 Peter 3:1–5)

Time and space won't allow a complete study of all the important concepts found in this passage. (More about that nasty word "submission" in chapter 4.) But central to the apostle's message is his concern to abolish the fear that he sees in the hearts of his readers. Did you notice those all-important phrases?

… the unfading beauty of a gentle, quiet spirit

… of great worth in God's sight

… do not give way to fear

In effect, Peter says to the wives he addresses, "Be the beautiful person God has created and recreated you in Christ Jesus to be. Be who you are. Don't put all kinds of pressure on yourself to argue your husband into the family of God. Don't feel compelled to pull out your intellectual stun-gun and talk him into surrender. Don't put all kinds of pressure on yourself to put up a strong facade. Don't throw up barricades of bravado in an effort to 'defend the faith.'

"Instead, remember how beautiful you are in God's sight. Remember the kindness and compassion the Holy Spirit is building in you. Remember who you are. Then relax and just be that person in your marriage."

No unbelieving husband is his wife's problem. No unbelieving wife is her husband's problem. An unbelieving or spiritually weak spouse is *God's* problem. Detach. Pray. Let God attract, entice, draw, court your partner. He wants to do that even more than you want to see it happen.

I Think It Was 1956 ...

Both David and Lucy are locked in uphill combat. Their lives, their marriages, their walk with the Lord—all include the kinds of challenges no one could envy.

Still, both of them have God-given strengths they need to celebrate. Lucy's mom, for example, encourages Lucy and prays for Lucy and her family. God has blessed Lucy with a pastor who cares, who listens, who has a keen insight into Lucy's hurts, and who is willing to take the time necessary to minister to her needs.

David has many friends in his congregation, friends who respect him, pray for him, and understand his pain. He has a wife who was once in the church and who, at least intellectually, understands foundational concepts such as sin and grace, forgiveness and eternal life.

What about you? What strengths has God given you? When was the last time you thanked Him for the strengths He has incorporated into your marriage and into your relationship with Him and other believers? When was the last time you celebrated those strengths? Don't let Satan blind you to the blessings, especially the spiritual blessings, your Lord has built into your life.

Before You Go On

1. Reread the working definition of spiritual loneliness from p. 24.

   a. Based on this definition and on the inventory you filled out as the chapter began, what events or ongoing situations can you personally identify as triggers for this kind of loneliness?

   b. When you are spiritually lonely, do you identify the experience in that way or do you tend to explain the discomfort in some other way? Explain.

   c. Would labeling spiritual loneliness as just that help you better cope with it? Explain.

2. Which of the approaches suggested to combat spiritual loneliness on pages 30–31 have you used? Which work best for you?

3. This chapter makes two coordinated points:

   Don't live in your family as if you had no church.

   Don't live in your church as if you had no family.

   a. What factors might make a Christian vulnerable to these temptations?

   b. Which of these pitfalls do you think is most likely to personally trip you up? Explain.

   c. What makes each of them so dangerous?

4. Have you ever struggled with the kinds of issues Lucy faces? Based on the Scriptures quoted in this chapter, what do you think Jesus would say to Lucy if He were to sit beside her and have a heart-to-heart talk?

5. Use the next page to list the strengths God has incorporated into your marriage and into your relationship with Himself and other believers. Concentrate on the areas listed below. Then plan a way to thank God for what He's done for you—an "out of the ordinary" way if you can. Write a song of thanksgiving and skip through the park singing it. Order a cake from the bakery and have them decorate it with the words, "Thanks, Jesus!" Buy a package of thank-you notes and send one to each person in your support system. Or … ???

The work the Holy Spirit has done in my heart from childhood on:

The support I have received and am now receiving from other believers in my earthly family and/or in my church family:

The evidence of openness or growth I've seen in my spouse's life, big or small:

3

WHAT ABOUT MY SPOUSE?

As I hung up the phone, my roommate threw me a look that would have wilted a bouquet of silk flowers. I did-n't understand her anger. I told her so. She just glared. I shrugged and walked away. We hadn't gotten along well— not for months. Bound together only by the financial neces-sity of sharing rent, we hadn't known one another when we signed a joint lease. It had been a mistake. From the start.

The morning after the phone call, I found a note on the kitchen table. Eight words: **What do you mean I'm not a Christian?**

Suddenly I saw. In my conversation the evening before, I had mentioned in passing that Tonya "wasn't a Christian." Insensitive? Probably, especially with Tonya right there in the room with me. It smacked of gossip and of spiritual arrogance, too, if I'm honest.

Nevertheless, it was true. Again and again I had lis-tened patiently while Tonya explained to me why she felt compelled to remain an agnostic. Why Jesus could not have been the Son of God. Why He could not have risen from the dead. How the early Christian church had corrupted an

ancient Babylonian rite to create Holy Communion. Tonya
ridiculed the most basic doctrines of the Christian faith.
How, then, could she object to my statement describing her
spiritual condition?

The Cultural Concept

What makes someone a Christian? If you accept our culture's shorthand definition, it's a person who's "nice," who doesn't rock anyone else's boat. Some people might broaden this definition a bit to include someone who acts morally. Still others might throw in some minimal standard of church attendance. Even so the focus remains outward, concentrated on behavior. To say someone "is not a Christian," then, can be interpreted as throwing rocks at their character, at their morals. It sounds judgmental rather than factual, nasty rather than diagnostic.

Because making the determination that someone is not a Christian carries such baggage, many believers shy away from admitting the true spiritual condition of their marriage partner. But as you think about your relationship with your spouse and about your own spiritual life, sooner or later you need to make an accurate diagnosis of his or her spiritual condition. Not to accuse. Not to judge. Not to hurt. But in order to align your feelings and your actions with reality and with the truths of God's Word. Otherwise your thinking will remain muddy and your decisions arbitrary. You will send contradictory messages in what you say and do.

Judging Hearts

When Jesus warned His disciples against judging others (Matt. 7:1–5), He put His finger on the sinful tendency to condemn others for their attitudes or actions. The key word here is condemn—to find fault, to criticize. That kind of judging hurts us. It hurts others. It damages our witness. It destroys relationships. It murders marriages.

But the Savior goes on in the very next breath to warn His disciples against "throw[ing] pearls to pigs." Most Bible commentators take this to mean that we should not keep on trying to share the precious Gospel message of grace and forgiveness for Jesus' sake with those who have shown they don't want to listen to us. Our Lord warns that if we do this, those to whom we speak will turn on us. They will "tear [us] to pieces" (Matt. 7:6). They will also trample our pearls underfoot. Their hearts will become even more hardened to the Savior's love.

In this mini-parable, Jesus shows that being non-judgmental has its limits. If we fail to make an accurate diagnosis of the spiritual condition of those to whom we witness, our failure can have dangerous consequences—both for us and for the unbeliever(s) we hope to touch with the precious Gospel.

Our Lord implies that we must make a judgment. We must determine whether or not the person to whom we could speak wants to hear what we have to say. If not, we don't condemn the person. We don't write him off. We don't stop caring about her. But neither do we blast away with both barrels, spewing out every Bible passage we've ever memorized to help us witness.

We don't condemn. We do make decisions about what to say and do and about what to pray based on sound judgment. We act and speak with wisdom and patience, wisdom and patience from God.

Perhaps you already know your partner's spiritual condition. Maybe he's made no secret of his atheism. Maybe she readily expresses her animosity toward God. Maybe your partner's coldness toward spiritual things registers close to absolute zero on the Kelvin scale.

On the other hand, perhaps matters aren't that clear-cut. Maybe you find it hard to tell yourself that your spouse is an unbeliever. Maybe you see an occasional spark of interest. Maybe he comes to church with you once in awhile—or even every Sunday. Maybe she has asked you to pray for her once or twice. Maybe he's more principled in his business than the Christian supervisor for whom you work. Maybe she's more moral than many of the Christian women you dated before marriage.

Even so, you must answer questions about your spouse's spiritual condition based on what the Scriptures say, not on his or her outward actions and not on your hopes or, worse still, your fears.

What does the Bible say? How does Scripture define saving faith? You already know the answer to that:

> *Whoever believes and is baptized will be saved, but whoever does not believe will be condemned.*
> (Mark 16:16)

Unbelief—and only unbelief—condemns. Refusing to receive God's gift of forgiveness and eternal life through Jesus the Savior condemns. Weak faith does not. As Isaiah wrote centuries ago, God is not interested in extinguishing the spark of faith in anyone's heart:

> *A bruised reed He will not break, and a smoking wick He will not snuff out.* (Is. 42:3)

God's concern for the weak in faith does not, however, negate what the rest of Scripture has to say about the definition of saving faith. The psalmist urges God's people, "Let the redeemed of the LORD say [so!] (Ps. 107:2).

Those who know Jesus as Savior say so. Maybe not always through a megaphone. Maybe not while standing on the corner of the busiest intersection in town. Maybe not always with thunderous conviction. But the redeemed of the Lord do say so:

> *If you confess with your mouth "Jesus is Lord," and believe in your heart that God raised Him from the dead, you will be saved. For it is with your heart that you believe and are justified, and it is with your mouth that you confess and are saved.* (Rom. 10:9–10)

Confession of faith does not, of course, save us. It's simply the evidence of the Holy Spirit's work, the fingerprints He leaves on human hearts He has turned toward God.

Can someone who does not believe in Jesus claim to have faith? Of course. As those outside the family of God are so quick to point out, the church on earth is full of hypocrites. Weeds will flourish beside the wheat in God's field until the day of harvest (Matt. 13:24–30). The "talk test" has never been 100% reliable and it never will be this side of heaven. But since we can apply this diagnostic tool in an unbiased way, it's the most reliable diagnostic tool the Scriptures give us.

If your spouse says, "Jesus is my Savior," you need to take that confession of faith as genuine. You dare not take on the role of a spiritual cardiologist, presuming to examine your partner's heart to determine whether or not saving faith resides there. On the other hand, if your partner does not make that confession, you dare not deny his or her spiritual deadness, no matter how moral his life, no matter how often she prays or attends church.

One last wrinkle. Sometimes a person will confess faith in Jesus Christ but will show no evidence of that faith relationship in his or her life. When the redeemed of the Lord say so, they say it with their lips but they say it by their actions too. Suppose someone claims to belong to Jesus but over an extended period of time, say many months or years ...

- Shows absolutely no interest in the things of God.

- Ignores every opportunity for worship and spiritual growth.

- Spends no time learning to know our Savior and His love more deeply.

- Knows God's will but shows no intention of obeying it.

What can we say about such a person's spiritual condition? Harsh as it may seem, we must conclude—with grief—that the individual does not know the Lord. As the apostle James pointed out to his first-century readers, faith without works is dead (James 2:17ff).

Works won't save, but saving faith works. Those

who love Jesus do, by His grace, bear the fruit of faith. Sometimes we see believers whose lives produce a sparse crop of fruit or fruit that is small and woody. Even so, we dare not deny the saving work of God in their hearts. But in the absence of fruit—particularly the kind of fruit in the list above—we must conclude that a particular branch remains unconnected to the Vine (John 15:1–6).

So what, you say. Why all this space devoted to deciding whether or not my spouse is in the faith or not, inside the family of God or outside of it? It boils down to this. If your marriage partner is an unbeliever and you ignore or deny that fact, you will at times excuse his actions and at other times blame him for those actions. You will continually bounce between anger and grief.

On the other hand, if your spouse is a believer who is weak in faith and you treat her as an unbeliever, you will at times find yourself excusing sin that needs to be confronted. You may miss opportunities to assure her of Christ's forgiveness, to fan the spark of faith that the Holy Spirit has ignited in her heart, to remind her of the Savior's love for her.

Accepting the situation, that is, acknowledging reality as it is and deciding to act in line with what you know rather than what you would like to believe, will protect you from the hurt that comes with unrealistic expectations. It will also help you avoid foolish mistakes in your patterns of relating to your spouse. You can't pretend your spouse into the Kingdom of God. You will hurt yourself (and probably him or her too) if you try.

Fears and More Fears

Unrealistic expectations can prove deadly in any relationship, especially in marriage relationships. If your partner is an unbeliever and if you can admit that fact to yourself, you will then be able to adjust the expectations you place on the relationship accordingly. You will also be better able to put yourself in your partner's place and to see through your partner's eyes at least some of the conflicts that will inevitably occur.

Many common conflicts that arise in marriages between believing and nonbelieving partners grow out of fear and feelings of inadequacy. In chapter 2 we looked at some of the things that trigger these emotions in Christian husbands and wives. Let's take a look at some of the factors that might lie beneath those same feelings in the heart of the unbelieving spouse.

Remember Craig from chapter 1? When he married Cynthia, both regarded the Christian faith with skepticism. Shortly after Cynthia came to faith, Craig began feeling uneasy about her new relationships—with both the Lord and her friends at church.

Some of Craig's fears are well-founded. Never again will Craig take first place in Cynthia's heart. That place is now—rightly—reserved for God Himself. Craig wonders how he can compete with God for Cynthia's loyalties. The answer is simply that he cannot. Because Craig loves Cynthia so much (in truth, idolizes her), the demotion to second place can't help but hurt. It arouses feelings of jealousy and anger, perhaps even rage, in Craig.

While Cynthia can't assume responsibility for the hurt Craig feels, she can help both herself and Craig if she recognizes his discomfort and the reason behind it. If the two of them can talk openly about their thoughts and feelings, chances are such discussion will help calm the storm raging inside Craig, although the winds will probably never die down completely unless and until Craig himself comes to saving faith.

Talking will probably also help resolve the antagonism Craig feels toward Cynthia's congregation and her relationships with the people there. Cynthia needs to realize that Craig very likely sees himself in direct competition with her new friends. They have something to offer her that he does not, and he knows it.

When Cynthia comes home excited about the closeness she feels with those in her prayer group, when she comes home enthused about the plans the education committee has made for this summer's vacation Bible school program, when she comes home thrilled with the insights her pastor shared in this morning's sermon, Craig will almost certainly flinch.

If the two do not address the situation head-on, Craig will find another way to express the turmoil he's feeling. He may respond coldly, ignoring her, and perhaps even retaliating by taking up a "hobby" of his own that will get him out of the house several nights of the week. Or he may respond hotly, nit-picking her involvement in congregational activities (e.g., "You said you'd be home at 9:00 and it's already 9:15. Where were you?").

Cynthia will do well to remember the possibility that Craig feels threatened by her relationships with her new Christian friends. She will do well to temper her enthusiasm around Craig. If the chairman of the education committee asks her to stop off at a restaurant for coffee after their meeting, she should almost certainly turn him down. Sensitive to Craig's concerns, Cynthia will ordinarily avoid any situation that could appear compromising.

Most important, however, Cynthia and Craig need to talk together about their feelings for each other. Cynthia may need to set some limits on the number of congregational activities in which she participates, both to convince Craig that she's not "becoming a nut" and to assure him that no other person or group of people will take his place in her heart.

While believers can feel spiritually lonely when cut off from intimacy with other Christians, all human beings experience emotional loneliness when they are ignored—intentionally or not. If Cynthia begins to spend night after night at church, Craig will soon feel abandoned. And rightly so. Love for Craig and concern for her relationship with him will lead Cynthia to set aside time just for him, time in which they can express and cultivate their love for one another.

On his part, Craig needs to recognize and express his feelings for Cynthia. He also needs to acknowledge, at least intellectually, Cynthia's need for Christian fellowship. If this does not happen, their relationship is headed for trouble.

"I Don't Get It"

Another reason for accurately diagnosing where your partner stands with the Lord Jesus lies in the words of St. Paul:

> *The man without the Spirit does not accept the things that come from the Spirit of God, for they are foolishness to him, and he cannot understand them, because they are spiritually discerned.* (1 Cor. 2:14)

Foolishness. That's the way an unbeliever would characterize much of the way God's people think and act. If your spouse does not know the Lord Jesus, he or she probably won't understand much of what goes on in your life:

- Your concern about his or her salvation.
- Your desire to give—both time and money—to your church.
- Your ideas about "right" and "wrong," especially your idea that these things are not relative but absolute.
- Your objection to certain cultural givens (e.g., pornography, media violence, cursing and swearing).
- Your joy in worship and the pleasure you take in Bible study and prayer.
- The intensity of your concern that your children grow up in the Christian faith.

Conflicts can erupt so easily over issues like these. When you find yourself in such a conflict, the easiest thing both partners can do is to withdraw into their respective corners and mutter to themselves about the unreasonableness of the other person. It's the easiest thing, but also the worst thing for the relationship.

The best thing, of course, is to talk the issue out.

As you do that, though, you need to keep in mind Paul's warning about spiritual discernment. Even if you explain your position with exceptional clarity and unimpeachable logic, you set yourself up for a fall if you expect your unbelieving partner to understand and agree with spiritual reasoning or scriptural principles.

Only when the Holy Spirit opens human hearts to His truth can we see that truth as anything but foolish. Those without the Spirit of God resident in their hearts do not (in fact, cannot) comprehend what we know to be true. If you find yourselves locked in dispute over clashing values, the only way out is summed up in the old adage about agreeing to disagree. Ideally you will come to that conclusion via a route of reciprocal respect.

In any case, after you've sorted through the feelings and dug down to the core issue, further argument or attempts to bludgeon one another into a change of heart will only lead to hurt feelings. A change of heart, you see, is precisely what the situation requires. The Holy Spirit regards heart surgery as His realm. And rightly so. You do best when you leave your spouse's heart in His tender care.

Talk? Or Walk?

Perhaps the most frustrating, the most confusing issue unbelieving partners must confront involves the inconsistency in their spouse's walk with the Lord. Why don't you live what you say? That question may form in your spouse's mind several times each week. Maybe several times each day.

That's not an indictment against you. In some cases, the question pops to mind because the unbelieving partner thinks a more consistent faith-walk on your part would make life easier for him, would take some pressure off her. But in most cases the question comes up because our culture has tied Christianity with right living.

In the minds of many people, being a Christian means being perfect—never feeling cranky, never losing one's temper, never worrying about health or finances, always acting considerately, always letting the other person have his/her way, always walking through the toughest situations with a smile.

Most believers feel dizzy as they read that description. We feel as though we walked into a kindergarten workbook exercise titled, "What's Wrong with This Picture?" Christianity, authentic Christianity, has little to do with "being nice." It has everything to do with being righteous. Because Jesus died and rose again for us, we have right standing with God. Our sins don't count against us in heaven's courtroom. We're forgiven and free to live as the holy people God declares us to be.

Sometimes our relationship with Christ means

confronting sin in others. Sometimes it means recognizing and expressing anger, frustration, and disgust at unjust situations around us—whether such an expression is "nice" or not. And too often, to our regret, we simply fail to live the holy lives we want to live in response to our Lord's love.

When we fail in relationships—in any relationship but especially our marriage relationship—we can only admit our failure. We can only accept responsibility. We can only apologize and ask for forgiveness from God and from our spouse. In our Lord's forgiveness we receive the power to go on living, minute by minute, in tune with His will.

Before You Go On

1. Spend some time prayerfully writing a paragraph or two describing in clear terms your perception of your spouse's spiritual condition and the evidence on which you have based your conclusions.

2. What problems have you encountered in your marriage by forgetting or denying what you've written in response to question 1?

3. What fears have disrupted your marriage relationship in the past? How? What might you do, under God, to help resolve these problems?

4. What basic differences in values most often

evoke conflict between you and your spouse? How have you handled these in the past. What happens when you agree to disagree? Who might help you think through these issues more clearly?

5. In what circumstances do you find it hardest to confess your sins to your spouse? How might taking a moment to remind yourself of God's unconditional love, forgiveness, and acceptance give you more courage in those situations where you need to apologize and ask for your spouse's forgiveness?

4

What about Our Marriage?

Highway construction crews seldom use fancy barricades when they set up roadblocks. Ordinary, dented barrels will do. It doesn't take fancy roadblocks to shut down communication in human relationships either. Time-worn barricades will do:

He won't ever talk; he just listens, shrugs, and walks away.

When we disagree, I feel too intimidated to say much. I just let issues build until the pile gets too high. Then I explode, and it's over until the next time.

She's so verbal. She just blows me out of the water. I don't know how to counter logic like hers. She talks and talks, but I don't think we'll ever communicate.

Relationship requires communication. Communication requires two willing participants. Both must care about themselves and about one another. Both must be willing to reveal thoughts and feelings, perhaps thoughts and feelings they have never dared share with anyone—risky business! Both must be willing to listen to the other person's words and to the feelings that lie behind the words. Again, risky business!

Sometimes—maybe often—hearing involves hurting. We may not want to see ourselves in the mirror of the other person's perceptions. Sometimes—maybe often—we hear and want to defend our position. Sometimes—maybe often—we hear and want to argue the logic of our own case instead of accepting and validating the other person's feelings.

But if both people in a given relationship want that relationship to grow, both must drop their other agendas. All their other agendas.

These basic principles of communication apply, of course, to any relationship. The more intimate the relationship, the more important the principles, and God designed no human relationship more intimate than marriage.

The Real Problem Is ...

You often hear it said at weddings, usually with a sigh—"Look, Hilda, aren't they just the perfect couple." Hilda may enjoy the romance of that thought, but both she and we know, of course, they aren't the perfect couple. There is no perfect couple. There is no perfect marriage. Anyone who enters a marriage relationship blissfully ignorant of the ups and downs certain to occur will come to a rude and blissless awakening, and not too many days or weeks after the I dos.

Disagreements, conflicts, and, yes, arguments will occur in every marriage. The importance of communication grows exponentially during times of conflict. When one or both partners refuse to talk about issues in contention, a relationship can deteriorate literally overnight. Remember what St. Paul wrote?

In your anger do not sin: Do not let the sun go down while you are still angry. (Eph. 4:26)

When we refuse to deal with anger God's way, we allow Satan to turn up the heat and stir the pot. Disagreements that once simply simmered soon come to a rolling boil and spill out all over the stove. Both partners get burned. The memory of that kind of pain lingers. Fearful of the heat, we avoid the kitchen. Communication becomes even less likely, the thought of it even more threatening.

Conflicts can escalate in any marriage. But conflict can take peculiar and uniquely destructive twists when one spouse is a Christian and the other is not. Remember Robert and Rachael from chapter 1? He's the school counselor, she the physician who had begun to take their two sons with her to the hospital on her Sunday morning rounds.

Robert has stuffed his feelings about the boys missing Sunday school deep inside. He knows that if he broaches the subject, Rachael's logic will be flawless. He knows she wants more time with her sons, and time in her life is at a premium right now. He knows he will never win an argument with her about the issue. He has never won anything significant before.

Now, though, a few weeks into the conflict, the focus of Robert's discomfort has begun to shift. He finds himself questioning Rachael's methods for disciplining the boys, or, perhaps more accurately, her lack of discipline.

Robert does a slow burn whenever he sees her ignore behavior he thinks should be addressed—and he's noticing more and more behavior like that all the time. He's as yet unaware of it, but in his mind the problem is taking on a growing spiritual aura.

Why can't Rachael understand the importance God places on respecting parents and others in authority? What will her easy-going attitude communicate to the boys about the Lord's attitude toward sin? How will the boys learn to treasure forgiveness if they never come to see the seriousness of disobedience?

Robert keeps asking himself questions like these, but he can't quite drum up the courage he needs to talk to Rachael.

Unless Robert acts soon, an issue that isn't necessarily a values conflict (disciplining the children) will become inextricably intertwined with an issue that really is one (their sons' church and Sunday school attendance). By ignoring the real problem, Robert has set about creating a new one, or so it would seem.

In one way, of course, all issues are spiritual issues for the Christian. We make all of our decisions in the light of our relationship with Jesus. We live out every aspect of our lives in light of the new creation we have become in Him (2 Cor. 5:17).

Even so, not all disagreements that arise in marriage require a to-the-death stand for the faith. We can easily find ourselves sucked into that stance, though, especially if we allow critical faith issues to burrow beneath the surface and lie there, unaddressed and unresolved.

Methods of disciplining the children can surely be one of these issues. The family budget may be another. Career decisions in-the-making by either partner may be a third. No one can furnish you with two lists of conflicts, one labeled "Clearly Spiritual" and the other labeled "Clearly Not." The point, though, is this: You need to ask the Holy Spirit for the wisdom to avoid taking spiritual offense when none has been given and for courage to address all conflicts head-on as they arise.

Don't Wait for a Crisis

The book of Proverbs stresses time and again the need for godly counsel and the wisdom we show when we seek it:

Let the wise listen and add to their learning, and let the discerning get guidance. (1:5)

The way of a fool seems right to him, but a wise man listens to advice. (12:15)

Pride only breeds quarrels, but wisdom is found in those who take advice. (13:10)

Plans fail for lack of counsel, but with many advisers they succeed. (15:22)

Listen to advice and accept instruction, and in the end you will be wise. (19:20)

How much plainer could our Lord have said it? How many more times need He repeat Himself? Why, then, do God's people so often find themselves threatened by the thought that they may need help in sorting out their relationship?

No marriage is as strong as it could be. No couple experiences all the intimacy they could experience. Most marriages—Christian marriages too—need work.

If, as you read this book, you are still in the first few months—the honeymoon stage—of marriage with someone whose spiritual life differs significantly from yours, you need to pray seriously about sitting down with a counselor now. You need to look for a forum in which you can work through issues that probably remained unaddressed in any premarital counseling you received.

Nearly all newly-weds need to practice experiencing and expressing honest feelings in ways that don't do permanent damage to their relationship. Unless each of you has honed the skills so necessary to resolve interpersonal conflict, you will also want to work on problem-solving and negotiating skills. In addition, if either of you grew up in a home where drugs or alcohol were abused, if you were sexually molested, or if either of you lived through the pain of your parents' divorce, you will almost certainly want to work through some of the trauma of those experiences (unless, of course, you have done so before now).

Just as crucially, you will want to think through and talk through important spiritual issues. (See pages 138–144 for a talk sheet that may help you open discussion with your spouse. While intended for singles contemplating marriage, the questions may prove helpful to married couples too.)

Don't wait for a crisis. Don't wait for the marriage to settle-in. After the first nine to 12 months, the direction of most relationships slips into automatic pilot. By that time, you and your partner will have developed an approach to conflict resolution, one that you will return to again and again by force of habit. Change will come much less easily once these patterns have developed. Seeking counsel now will enable you to set them by design, not default.

Perhaps none of this talk about conflict resolution and communicating feelings sounds especially "spiritual" to you. If so, you need to remind yourself that *all* real wisdom, *all* true insight, *all* workable interpersonal skills come to us from our Creator. God understands all about human psychology. In fact, He invented it.

All couples need to understand and use basic communication skills. All couples need to understand and practice being more aware of their emotions and expressing those emotions in mutually helpful ways. But in a marriage between a Christian and an unbeliever, these understandings and skills become even more critical. The better you and your partner master the skills, the better you understand one another's personality and emotions, the better equipped you will be to address spiritual conflicts when they (inevitably) arise.

All this talk about seeking counsel may conjure up the question of where and how to find help. How can you find someone competent? Should you look for a "Christian" or for a "secular" counselor? How will you pay for counseling?

Ideally, you and your spouse met with your pastor for several premarital counseling sessions. If so, and if both of you felt comfortable as you worked together, give serious thought to returning there for postmarital counseling.

But what if your pastor does not feel qualified to do follow-up counseling? What if for one reason or another he doesn't have time? What if your spouse felt awkward counseling with *your* pastor? What if you and your spouse find yourselves in your sixth year of marriage rather than your sixth month and the problems between you have escalated to a point that you're uncertain about your pastor's ability to help you? What then?

In most cases, you could ask your pastor to refer you to someone trustworthy, qualified, skilled. Many times pastors initiate and maintain working relationships with Christian psychologists or social workers. Sometimes, the two professionals work jointly, the couple seeing the pastor one week and the psychologist the next.

But suppose no Christian counselor is available. Suppose you or your spouse question the credentials or the skills of the Christians in your area who counsel. Is it dangerous or wrong for a believer to use a secular counselor?

Not in and of itself. Some believers fear secular counselors, convinced that the advice they give may contradict the Christian faith. The truth is that most credentialed psychologists, psychiatrists, and social workers treat clients professionally.

A truly professional counselor will respect your faith, will not challenge or belittle it. A truly professional counselor will not try to convert you to the Church of Scientology or convince you of the merits of Transcendental Meditation or argue you into seeing the superiority of Buddhism vis-a-vis Christianity. Neither you nor your spouse have asked for that. And both you and the counselor know it.

You need not feel disloyal to your Lord nor to your church should you and your spouse decide to look for help from a secular counselor. Psychologists have set themselves the task of exploring a specific aspect of God's creation—human behavior. They study a specific cluster of characteristics our Creator has built into His human creatures. It's not wrong for God's children to take advantage of their discoveries and skills. When we do so, we simply act on what we say we believe each time we repeat the Apostles' Creed, "I believe in God, the Father Almighty, maker of heaven and earth." God looked at everything He made and pronounced it good. Can we contradict His evaluation?

Two practical keys to finding competent help:

- *Look for someone with excellent professional credentials and also a good clinical reputation, someone who has helped others, perhaps even someone you know.*

Again, your pastor may help point you in the right direction. Or perhaps someone else you know and trust from your congregation has worked successfully with a specific professional and would be willing to refer you.

- *Interview potential counselors.* Don't just choose the name that happens to appear at the top of the list you've compiled. When you call for an appointment, explain that you'd like a 10- to 15-minute interview. Take a list of questions along, a list you and your spouse have generated together. Ask about training, professional certification, and the person's preferred approach to marital counseling. Include questions that apply specifically to your needs or circumstances too. Interview two or three counselors, more if need be. Compare their answers to your questions. Keep looking until you find a person on whom you can both agree, one with whom both you and your spouse feel comfortable and confident.

One warning: Even after you have done all you can to ensure you'll be able to trust the counselor you've chosen, you need to remember that no Christian can abdicate responsibility for his or her own spiritual welfare to another person. If you question a counselor's techniques, if you wonder about a counselor's advice, if you doubt the morality of a counselor's suggestions or feel fearful that the recommendations you have received will damage your faith, by all means talk to your pastor. Don't just go along to get along. Doing that would be spiritually dangerous and irresponsible.

But What If ...

- *My spouse won't go along?* Then go alone. The only person you can change is you anyway. If you believe your marriage needs help and your spouse refuses to take part in pursuing that help, his or her refusal only proves your point—the relationship needs help.

Be aware that by looking for outside intervention in your own life and by seeking out people who can help you discover how to live more comfortably with yourself and with others, you have begun to change the relational system that exists between you and your spouse. The relationship will never be quite the same again. Your partner will almost certainly resist the changes you are making, perhaps subtly, perhaps head-on. But you must make those changes—for your own good and for the good of your marriage, even if your partner doesn't see it that way right now. Even if your partner never sees it that way.

- *We can't afford it?* The answer to that question is a cliché that is nonetheless true: You can't afford not to do it. If you see your pastor for help, there will almost certainly be no fee at all. If you go outside your church, check to see if your medical insurance will cover some of the expenses. Many community-based or denomination-based mental health services set fees on a sliding scale.

Actively pursue the help you need. It's critical for your faith and also for your family. Most important of all, pray that the Lord will lead you to a counselor who can help you become more fully the person He's created you to be in Christ.

The S Word

If you've read this far, and if you've come out of certain theological or denominational traditions, and especially if you're a woman, alarm bells have probably rung for you more than once as you've read this chapter. You may be asking questions such as:

But what about submission?

Aren't wives supposed to obey their husbands no matter what?

Isn't some of what you're talking about gross rebellion?

Yes. I plead guilty. And unabashedly so. I believe that the Scriptures teach about godly submission in marriage. But just as surely as godly submission exists, so does godly rebellion. Just as there is such a thing as ungodly rebellion, so also there is such a thing as ungodly submission.

Let's look at that, keeping in mind the basic principles introduced in chapter 1. Remember especially principle 4—*God's truth, spoken in love, can help.*

Let's search the Scriptures and put together a fuller picture of what godly submission means in the context of marriage, particularly in the kind of spiritually mixed marriages we have been talking about. We'll do that in the next chapter.

Before You Go On

1. How would you describe your usual pattern of communication in your marriage? How would you describe that of your spouse? Give an example of each.

2. Do those patterns change during conflict? If so, how? If not, do they intensify? Give an example.

3. How satisfied are you with the patterns you've just described?

4. How would you evaluate the effect these patterns of communication are having on your marriage?

5. What kinds of counseling have you experienced in the past? (Include formal and informal experiences.) How helpful were those experiences? Explain.

6. What kinds of help are you getting now? From whom? What else could you do to get help with the areas of conflict in your marriage? How would your spouse react to these courses of action? How do you know?

7. Has this chapter provoked a desire to do something more to help yourself or your marriage? How will you follow through on that? When will you do it?

5

WHAT ABOUT SUBMISSION AND MY WITNESS?

Few scriptural concepts have been contorted more grotesquely than the concept of submission in marriage. Those on the far left of the feminist movement have caricatured a submissive Christian wife as little better off than a galley slave in a Charleton Heston movie. Ignorant. Barefoot. Beaten. Helpless. A sex object.

Sad to say, some on the fringes of the Christian church have fueled the feminists' fire. Women in these churches have been taught that to please God they must accept any insult their husband chooses to fling at them or at their children. They must cater to his every whim, no matter how hurtful. They must "win their spouse for Christ" by giving in to marital rape or other gross physical abuse.

In short, they must let him have his way—in everything—no matter how damaging his way may prove to be physically, emotionally, economically, or spiritually.

This view twists a holy reality into something evil, a demonic parody of God's will. Like a fun house mirror at some amusement park in hell, it warps and deforms God's intended blessing beyond recognition. Our heavenly Father must weep when He sees the people He so loves damaged and sometimes even destroyed by devilish lies like these.

Submit to What?

Because the word submission and the concept that lies behind it carries such heavy emotional baggage, especially as it has been applied to the proper role of husbands and wives, let's back away from it a bit, at first. Instead of looking at how the submission can work in a Christian's marriage, let's look first at how it works for God's people in other relationships.

Take submission to governmental authorities, for example. Here's what Paul wrote to the believers in Rome:

*Everyone must **submit** himself to the governing authorities, for there is no authority except that which God has established.*

The authorities that exist have been established by God. Consequently, he who rebels against the authority is rebelling against what God has instituted, and those who do so will bring judg-

ment on themselves.

For rulers hold no terror for those who do right, but for those who do wrong.

Do you want to be free from fear of the one in authority? Then do what is right and he will commend you. **For he is God's servant to do you good.** (Rom. 13:1–3, emphases added)

The word *submit* in the first sentence has the same root as the word *submit* used in the New Testament passages that talk about wives submitting to husbands. Two points critical for a discussion of submission lie imbedded in the text:

- God expects His people to submit to authority, in this case to obey the law and to respect government officials. He says that He Himself has ordained the authority governments exercise. Governing authorities act as God's representatives.

- God also reminds us that He gives authority to government for the good of the governed. It's His gift to us. He intends it to be a good gift. He's given it for our benefit.

Most of us chafe from time to time at the thought of this kind of submission. Perhaps we're in a hurry and we fume at the 45 mph speed limit posted in the construction zone we find ourselves passing through. Or maybe we snort as we read about yet another example of monumental government waste and then hear our accountant tell us that we owe an additional $376 in income taxes.

Still, we concede that we're better off under the government's authority than we would be under the chaos of anarchy. So we submit. Specifically, we ease up on the accelerator. We write out the check to the IRS. At least most of the time.

Paul's words to the church in Rome regarding submission to the authority of the state seem absolute. But are they? One basic principle of biblical interpretation is that in order to understand what the Bible says about a particular topic, we must look at everything the Bible teaches about that topic. Our goal in doing that is not to look for rules, but to tune the receiver of our hearts so that we can hear the heart of God as He speaks to us in His Word. We want to align our lives with His will for us, knowing that He loves us and wants the very best for us.

Remember the day the apostles stood before the religious authorities in Jerusalem? They had dived—almost eagerly, it seems—into hot water with these religious authorities (who served also as civil authorities at the time). These authorities had forbidden anyone to teach or to heal in the name of Jesus. The apostles had done both anyway, and with results that drew plenty of publicity.

Listen to the exchange of fire between the two groups:

> "We gave you strict orders not to teach in this name [the name of Jesus]," [the authorities] said. "Yet you have filled Jerusalem with your teaching and are determined to make us guilty of [Jesus'] blood."
>
> Peter and the other apostles replied: "We must obey God rather than men!
>
> "The God of our fathers raised Jesus from the dead—whom you had killed by hanging Him on a tree. God exalted Him to His own right hand as Prince and Savior that He might give repentance and forgiveness of sins to Israel.
>
> "We are witnesses of these things, and so is the Holy Spirit, whom God has given to those who obey Him."
>
> When they heard this, they were furious and wanted to put them to death. (Acts 5:28–33)
>
> "We must obey God rather than men!"

Ungodly rebellion? Or godly defiance? Who can question that Peter and the others did the right thing in refusing to obey the governing authorities? Submission to government, while a godly thing, has its limits. What are they? Peter could scarcely have framed the principle with more clarity: Obedience to God takes precedence over submission to human authority.

Everywhere the word submission appears in the New Testament, we see the admonition to submit tempered by the limitation that we owe ultimate submission only to God Himself. Human authority has its limits. No matter what the relationship, the same principle pops up:

- We are enjoined to submit to spiritual leadership and told that God entrusts authority to our spiritual leaders for our good (e.g., Heb. 13:7, 17). Still, spiritual leaders who run amok must be confronted (e.g., Gal. 2:11ff.; 1 Tim. 5:17–20).

- Children are told to submit to the authority of their parents, just as Jesus Himself submitted to Mary and Joseph, imperfect and sinful though they were (Luke 2:51; Eph. 6:1–3). Even so, parents are commanded not to exasperate their children but to nurture them and train them in the Lord (Eph. 6:1ff.).

While we can't go into all the passages pertinent to the point here, we can summarize several important truths:

- In every instance, those who exercise God's

authority also carry a load of responsibility. Our Lord holds authorities accountable to Himself.

- In every instance, those who submit to authority can expect, on the authority of God's Word and promises, to receive blessings because of their submission.

- In every instance, submission has its limits.

Rebellion can be rightly termed godly rebellion whenever someone to whom God has given authority demands disobedience to God. Not only may we rebel. We must rebel. We must obey God rather than men, just as the apostles did.

The wife whose husband demands that she sign a fraudulent income tax return must refuse to submit, must insist on either correcting the return or on filing a separate return (Matt. 22:21).

The wife whose husband forbids her to attend public worship, to read the Scriptures, or to teach their children about Jesus must refuse to submit, must insist on obeying God (Ps. 75:5–8; Heb. 10:25; Deut. 11:18ff.).

The wife whose husband insists that she watch pornographic movies with him in an effort to enhance their sexual enjoyment must refuse to submit, must insist on obeying God (Eph. 5:3–8; Phil. 4:8).

The examples given here fall definitively under

the principle of "obeying God rather than men." But clear-cut cases like these aren't the only ones in which we as God's people must choose to submit to Him rather than to human beings.

When the Water Gets Muddy

Up to this point in the discussion, we've considered primarily the submission wives give or must refuse to give unbelieving husbands. Let's broaden the topic now to include Christian husbands married to unbelieving wives.

Paul spoke to both wives and husbands as he wrote:

> Submit to one another out of reverence for Christ.

The apostle then goes on to command wives to submit to their husbands and husbands to show the same self-sacrificial love to their wives that Christ showed when He died on the cross for His Bride, the church. These commands seem absolute, just as the commands about submission to government recorded for us in Romans 13 do. But are they? Does submission in marriage have its limits?

I believe the Scriptures clearly draw a line at which godly submission to human authority ends and righteous submission to God's divine authority begins. We can sketch a map that shows where that line falls across the terrain of marriage by saying something like this:

> *Those who belong to Jesus Christ need not and must not submit at any time when anyone says or does anything that demeans our personhood as God's redeemed children or that damages the work that the Holy Spirit is doing in our hearts to convince us of the identity He has given us in Christ and of our infinite value in His eyes.*

What does that mean in practical terms? For example, if someone tells us we are worthless; calls us demeaning names; or ridicules our bodies, our intelligence, our faith, our feelings, or our actions, we need not and we must not submit. We need not and we probably should not remain engaged in that conversation. In fact, we need not remain in that person's presence. We must not choose to allow ourselves to be insulted, hurt, debased, or shamed in these ways.

Neither need we—nor should we—submit to any kind of physical harm. No one under the guise of "godly authority" has the right to hit, slap, punch, shake, or push another person. To go further, no one has the right to cut you, to burn you, to give you a black eye, or to break any of your bones. No one has the right to force intercourse on you, to force you to submit to oral sex, or to make you perform any other sexual act to which you object.

How unnecessary it ought to be to state such obvious truths, especially when writing to God's people. But some—sad to say, even some leaders—in the church have so distorted passages like Ephesians 5 and 1 Peter 3 that Satan himself could hardly have written a more demonic rule book for behavior in marriage.

Remember principle 1 from chapter 1? *You are important to God.* Our heavenly Father does not shrug it off when another human being chooses to hurt one of His children. He has said:

> *Whoever touches you touches the apple of [My] eye.* (Zech. 2:8)

In plain English, whoever hurts one of God's kids pokes the King of the universe in the eye. Not a small thing. Not an infraction He will likely overlook.

But let's go back to the statement that began this part of our discussion:

> *Those who belong to Jesus Christ need not and must not submit at any time when anyone says or does anything that demeans our personhood as God's redeemed children or that damages the work that the Holy Spirit is doing in our hearts to convince us of the identity He has given us in Christ and of our infinite value in His eyes.*

What biblical basis can we cite to support this

contention? In his first letter to the Christians at Corinth, Paul explained that God's people collectively form God's building; together we make up the New Testament temple in which He has chosen to dwell (1 Cor. 3:5–17).

Paul goes on to explain that this temple grows as His faithful ministers build on the only solid foundation—the person and the work of Jesus Christ Himself. Faithful builders build with gold, silver, and precious stones—the pure Word of God, His Word to us of Law and Gospel, of sin and grace.

By contrast, some try to use worthless building materials—the wisdom of mere human opinion. Just as no master builder would choose to construct a cathedral with sticks and straw, so those who try to build God's temple, God's Church, with human ideas will find their work burned up in the fires of the final judgment.

Worse still, and this is the point that relates to our present discussion, some of those on the construction site don't build at all. Instead, they destroy. They tear down what Christ wants to build up:

> *Don't you know that you yourselves are God's temple and that God's Spirit lives in you? If anyone destroys God's temple, God will destroy him; for God's temple is sacred, and you are that temple.* (1 Cor. 3:16–17)

Some destroyers disguise themselves as theologians, as shepherds, as pastors. But they preach their own words, not God's Word. They harp on human deeds and urge us somehow to make ourselves acceptable to God.

Other destroyers have no religious credentials. They do not shroud their destructive words and actions in a cloak of piety. Still, they do Satan's destructive work in Christian hearts. They lie to us believers about who we are. They condemn. They accuse. They question or deny our worth. They shame us. They tell us—in words and in actions—that we are something other than God's blood-bought children.

Now it's true that the text addresses the whole church ("you yourselves"—plural). Does that mean that Paul writes here only about actions that wreck that church collectively, that attack the one, Holy Christian Church?

Let's answer that question with another question. How is it that Christ's church usually suffers damage? Isn't it one stone at a time? One martyr at a time? One believer at a time? Doesn't Satan usually apply his sledgehammer to God's edifice brick by brick?

This analogy is even more far-reaching. The Holy Spirit lives in each one of God's people. His presence unites us not only with God but also with one another. His presence unites each of us with all of us. We're connected. We belong to each other in the church. Our strength in the Lord is a strength the Spirit creates in individual hearts to be sure. But because of our unity in the Spirit, it's a joint strength as well.

Therefore, anything that diminishes your understanding of God's love for you and your conviction about the reality and the depth of that love also diminishes me. It weakens the whole body of Christ.

For these reasons, any believer whose confidence in the Lord's love for him or her is being damaged need not—and must not—submit to that abuse. She must leave the conversation. He must leave the room. And if the damaging words or actions continue over an extended period of time, he/she may need to leave the relationship.

Is it that serious? Yes.

It's a matter of God's glory in Christ Jesus in His church.

It's a matter of God's concern for you as an individual.

It's a matter of life and death—spiritual life and death.

Seek Counsel

The principles are fairly clear. Their application is sometimes less so. When does legitimate confrontation in a relationship become illegitimate accusation? When does truth-telling become name-calling? When do reasonable requests become devilish demands?

Embroiled in the heat of the moment, we can't always tell. No matter how much we've grown in the Lord, no matter how spiritually mature or emotionally together we may be, we won't always be able to sort out questions like these, especially during times of ongoing turmoil.

We need one another in the church at times like that. The counsel of mature believers and of our pastor takes on special importance during crises in relationships as important as the marriage relationship.

If you find yourself hurt and confused, talk to brothers and sisters in Christ whom you trust. Show them this chapter if you need to. Lay out the facts of your situation as you see them and let them react from a less-biased perspective. Ask for help, but not for help in making rules (e.g., "I will submit if he says X, but not Y"; "I will submit to action X, but not Y").

Rule-making, you see, is dangerous. Not all situations are alike, even if the details are carbon copies of one another. Just because Mary Smith could do thus and so in her relationship with her husband does not necessarily mean that you can. You're not Mary Smith. You haven't had her experiences, her hurts, her opportunities.

Instead of setting rules, ask for help in understanding the whole counsel of His Word, in listening to His heart of love as that love is recorded for us in the Holy Scriptures, in discovering His principles from those Scriptures that apply in your situation.

Two key truths that may help as you explore:

- God is faithful; He will give you all the strength you need to do His will, to show His love, to be His witness.

- God loves you; He wants you to protect yourself (and your children) physically, emotionally, and spiritually, using the good sense and spiritual discernment He's given you.

Godly decisions lie balanced across both those beams of truth.

Yes, But ...

I've defined submission to this point in the negative by laying out what it is not. I chose to do this for what I believe are good reasons. The concept is so highly charged, both in the church and in the world, that most people cannot listen rationally to a positive definition until all the straw men have bitten the dust.

So now that we've seen what submission is not, let's look at what submission does involve in a godly, biblical sense. Let's explore it especially as it applies in marriages in which only one partner has a relationship with Christ Jesus as Savior.

Submit to One Another

God commands Christian husbands and wives, "Submit to one another out of reverence for Christ" (Eph. 5:21). In everyday language, we might use words like these:

- Get along with each other.
- Don't insist on exercising your "rights."
- Don't inflate every little incident into a federal case.
- Don't buy the myth that your relationship should always be 50–50. Sometimes it will be 40–60; sometimes 60–40.
- Be willing to let your relationship be 0–100 or 100–0 at times when that's necessary because of weakness in your spouse or in yourself.

Look for your partner's good qualities. Remind yourself—often—of what you saw as you looked into your bride's eyes the day you stood beside her and said, "I do." Remember what you heard in your fiancé's voice that night he asked you to spend your life with him and you answered, "I will."

In short, if your husband or wife makes a request that does not involve disobedience to God or damage to you, yield to it—even if you don't especially feel like doing so.

Knowing Christ's forgiving love and relying on

His Spirit's power, submit to your partner. Submit because of your reverence for Christ. Because of **your** reverence for Christ, even if your spouse does not share that reverence.

Husbands, Love Your Wives

You know how that command ends: Love your wives *as Christ loved the church and gave Himself [for it]* (Eph. 5:25). How did Christ love the church? Self-forgetfully. Self-sacrificially. Doing what was best for us, even when it meant the cross.

Jesus did not wait to love us until we submitted to Him. He did not wait to love us until we loved in return. He did not wait to love us until we believed the right things, said the right things, thought the right things, or did the right things. He loved—and died—while we were still sinners (Rom. 5:8).

In short, husbands are to do whatever they can (within the limits set down earlier) to meet the needs of their wives. If you are a Christian husband, be Jesus to your wife. Put her needs ahead of your own. Knowing Christ's forgiving love and relying on His Spirit's power, love your wife as Christ loves His bride, His church. Love her because **you** know Christ's love, even if she does not yet know that love.

Wives, Submit to Your Own Husbands ...

You know how that command ends: Wives, submit to your own husbands, *as to the Lord* (Eph. 5:22). Other Scriptures make it clear that God holds husbands ultimately responsible for the management and welfare of the family. This is true whether a husband knows and believes it or not.

Still, a wise husband will listen to his wife. Wise wives will share their wisdom with their husbands. If both partners commit themselves to communicating their ideas and feelings and if they apply wise problem-solving techniques to difficult decisions, impasses will occur only rarely.

But when a disagreement cannot be resolved, our Lord wants Christian wives to yield, to submit *as to the Lord*. Within the limits set down earlier in this chapter, wives are to do this whether their husband is "nice" or not. Whether he does everything perfectly or not. Whether she agrees with his every decision or not. A Christian wife is not to submit grudgingly. Not with an eye toward finding loopholes. But with a heart made willing by Jesus' love for her. God will bless such submission. He will do so even if the decision turns out later to have been wrong.

In short, if you're a Christian wife, communicate. Participate. Make your opinion known in a winsome way. Pray that God will give your husband wisdom to meet his responsibilities for the family welfare. Then, knowing Christ's forgiving love and relying on His Holy Spirit's power, yield to your husband's decisions. Do everything in your power to make sure they produce a positive outcome. Support your husband and yield to him as you would to Christ Jesus Himself. Do this because of *your* relationship with Jesus, whether or not your husband is submitted to Christ.

Who Knows?

It does happen. It has happened. God wants it to happen. He wants it even more than you do. God wants to draw your spouse to Himself in saving faith. After all, Jesus died for your husband, for your wife. The Holy Spirit is even now at work, softening hearts, looking for opportunities, bringing witnesses across the paths of unbelievers.

God has used Christian wives to win their husbands. God has used Christian husbands to win their wives. Remember Craig and Cynthia?

Cynthia had gone back to church and had gotten involved with a vengeance. So much so that Craig worried for several months about whether she'd become a fire-breathing fanatic.

In the months and years that followed, Cynthia tuned-in to Craig's fears. Finding support and guidance from her pastor and her friends at church, she backed away from the confrontational style she had initially used when she talked with him about the Savior. Instead, she listened more. She gently reminded him of her prayers for him. And she did pray, just as she told him she did.

It took eight years. The Holy Spirit hammered at Craig's heart all that time. Two weeks before Craig and Cynthia celebrated their 10th wedding anniversary, Craig lost his job. Cynthia took many deep breaths to steady herself during the six months of unemployment that followed. She didn't always do or say the right things.

Still, Cynthia lived out her faith during that difficult time. She regularly reminded Craig of her love for him and of his importance to her. She assured him of her support whenever he went for an interview and especially when those interviews failed to result in job offers. She let him know of her redoubled prayers for him. She looked for support from other believers, and kept looking until the Lord led her to Christians who would listen to her, encourage her, and pray with her.

In short, at a time when she could have fallen apart, she relied on God's grace and in doing so became a source of strength for Craig. Later on, he admitted that her courage amazed him. And he knew it was not coming from inside her because she told him so.

In the end, though, God used not Cynthia but the husband of one of her friends to lead Craig to faith. Cynthia and Linda had gone shopping together one evening while Craig and Kendall stayed home to replace the brake pads on Craig's car.

Afterward, neither Craig nor Kendall could say for sure how their conversation about Jesus had begun. Some-

where along the line, though, it had. Craig had asked questions. Kendall had answered. By the time the two had popped the last hub cap back in place, the Holy Spirit had done His faith-creating work.

Cynthia felt temporarily jealous. She had always hoped to be the one to pray with Craig that first time he thanked Jesus for His gift of salvation.

"But I understand how it might have been hard for Craig to listen to me talk about that," she now admits. "We may be just too close for me to have explained everything and for him to have asked what he needed to ask."

She pauses, then goes on, "It's different now. Better— in lots of ways. But our relationship hasn't yet changed in all the ways I want it to. We still don't pray much together, Craig and I.

"In some ways it was easier before. When Craig did or said something that hurt me, I told myself that he didn't understand, that he couldn't really understand. He was a dead man—spiritually dead, I mean.

"I don't mean to sound judgmental. It was just the truth. The Bible says that those who don't know the Lord ... well, they're spiritually dead. So, I figured, what can I expect from a dead man?

"Now, thank God, he's alive. But we still hurt each other sometimes. It's hard. Disappointing, really. With God's help though, we're working on it.

"We're not where I know God wants us to be. Not yet. But we're not where we were either. I keep hoping, asking *the Lord to change us. To change us both.*

"The main thing I'd say to someone whose partner doesn't know Jesus? Get support from other Christians. Lots of support. Be patient. Keep on praying. Keep on living out your faith. And don't give up. There's hope—in God."

Before You Go On

1. Before you read this chapter, how would you have defined submission?

2. Has your definition changed? If so, how? If not, why not?

3. Paul wrote to all of us as believers, "Submit to one another out of reverence for Christ" (Eph. 5:21). When do you find it easiest to yield to your partner's needs or wants? When do you find it hardest? What does that tell you about yourself? About your relationship?

4. How does knowing Jesus' forgiveness and love for you take the pressure off you to drum up a submissive spirit inside yourself through your own power? What's the alternative to trying harder to love and submit? (See Phil. 3:14.)

5. Is any part of your relationship with your spouse abusive? If so, who could help you think through what you need to do to call a halt to that abuse? When will you talk to that person?

6. How did you react to the story of Craig's conversion? Did it give you hope? Did it cause you to rethink any of your expectations? Explain.

6

WHAT ABOUT THE KIDS?

Gordon's mom found him crying in the darkness long after he should have been asleep. "What *is* going on here?" Mom wondered. Gordon's teacher had phoned earlier that afternoon, concerned about Gordon's recent penchant for picking playground fights and his seeming inability to concentrate in class. Now this.

Puzzled, Mom cracked the door open just far enough so that the light from the hallway would illuminate Gordon's bed. Then she sat down on the edge and handed the 10-year-old a tissue she had pulled from the box on his dresser.

"What's up, Bud?" she asked.

Gordon just looked at her, tears filling his eyes once more.

Mom tried again. "You've had a rough couple of weeks, huh?"

Gordon sniffed and nodded. A long pause. Then his body began to jerk in silent sobs. "I ... I don't want ... to go to heaven ... if Jeff can't ... can't be there too."

Jeff, Gordon's step-dad, had married Gordon's mother

a few months before. Gordon, devastated by the tragic death of his biological father five years earlier, had eyed Jeff warily at first, afraid to trust, afraid to love again. Jeff, a longtime Little League coach and a natural with boys, hadn't pushed.

In fact, it was Jeff's idea that Gordon call him Jeff, not Dad. Gordon had lowered the drawbridge of his heart ever so slowly. But by the day of the wedding, Jeff had walked across that bridge directly into Gordon's heart.

As Mom listened that night, Gordon spilled out his thoughts and fears like so many pieces of a giant jigsaw puzzle. Life. Death. Heaven. Hell. He talked about the Savior. About the Savior whom Jeff respectfully—but firmly— rejected. When Gordon fell silent, all the pieces had fallen into place. Mom saw the burden that had weighed so heavily on Gordon's heart.

The conversation that night was the first in a series that would stretch across the coming decades as Gordon and his mom worried, prayed, and cried together.

The Hardest Thing

As I researched this book, I spoke with dozens of people about the dilemmas they face in their spiritually mixed marriages. Again and again I listened as people described the dilemma of how to respond to their children's questions and concerns. Nearly every parent with whom I talked mentioned conflict with their spouse about the children as a major problem.

In most cases, parents identified this as THE major problem they faced.

The questions lie across the total spectrum of life's experiences. They involve the activities and daily rituals that set a home's spiritual tone:

- Shall we pray meal prayers or not? If so, will Dad/Mom participate? What about bedtime prayers? Family devotions?

- What kinds of language may adults use in our home? Children? If there's a double-standard, how will we explain it?

- What movies will we see as a family? What TV programs and videos will we watch? How will we decide what's suitable and what's not? Who will explain the reasons behind our choices to our children? How will these reasons be explained?

- How will we address other moral questions? How will we deal with situations in which Mom's values and morals differ from Dad's?

- Will the children attend church with Mom/Dad? Will the unchurched parent come along? If so, what will the children be told about his/her attendance? If not, how will we explain it?

- If Mom/Dad worships in another, non-Christian faith (e.g., Mormon, Jewish, Islam, Baha'i), will the children ever attend services with that parent? If so, how will that faith be explained in a way that does not create confusion? If not, how can we teach the child(ren) respect for that parent's faith?

- Will the children attend a Christian school? a private school? a public school? Can each parent support this decision with a clear conscience?

Parenting Is Not for Ostriches

Issues like these beg to be addressed. Ignored, they will never go away. Like mushrooms in a dark, humid cellar they will grow. Ideally, parents will discuss issues like these before they become parents. Even better, they will discuss them before they become husband and wife. Yet if you and your spouse have not talked about these issues before, it's not too late. Take time to do it now. The sooner the better. When your children enter their preteen years, discussion will still be possible, but not nearly so easy. Take advantage of the glow most couples share when they first find out they are pregnant.

Talk to one another early and often. A single, "magic talk" will not suffice. You will need to keep on talking because as the children grow, the issues will change. New conflicts will arise. New questions will come up. Keep on communicating with each other.

Relativity Revisited

What kinds of conflict can you expect? Most issues will orbit somewhere around the elusive sphere of moral relativism. When Albert Einstein first formulated his theory of relativity, he did so in an attempt to define relationships between velocity, time, and mass in the physical world.

Little could Einstein have guessed that his ideas about the material universe would be transmuted into theories of cultural relativism. Little could he have known that we would find ourselves a few decades later living in a society that for the most part scoffs at the notion of absolute truth. But here we are nevertheless.

Christianity stands in stark contrast to many cultural norms. Christians reject notions such as these:

- Those who sincerely believe in God have His favor, even apart from Jesus Christ and His saving work on the cross.

- If someone honestly tries to live a good life, God will accept that effort as sufficient.

- A loving God could not condemn anyone to eternal punishment in a literal place like hell.

- Jesus was a great teacher, a wonderful man like Buddha and Mohammed, who taught His followers how to live a God-pleasing life.

- Obeying Jesus' teachings is one of the many ways to achieve peace with God.

- The Ten Commandments grew out of a much simpler, less sophisticated culture than ours. In fact, the whole idea of "sin" is outmoded when one considers what we now know, especially in the fields of psychology and sociology.

- Any moral question can be answered adequately with three simple words, "It all depends."

Approval vs. Respect

Do you remember the apostle Paul's conversation with the intellectuals who met each day in Athens on Mars Hill? (See Acts 17:21ff.) The Bible tells us that many of the citizens of that city and the foreigners who visited there spent their time doing nothing but "talking about and listening to the latest ideas." Paul's audience had never heard of Einstein. Yet many of them would have swallowed whole today's theories of moral and spiritual relativism.

Paul addressed an audience arguably as sophisticated and as educated as people in our culture today. He spoke politely, quoting from one of the Greek poets and even complimenting the Athenians' interest in theology.

"Men of Athens!" he began, "I see that in every way you are very religious." He went on from there, though, to declare that truth could be known, the truth that God has revealed about Himself in Jesus Christ. Paul verbally demolished not only the reality of the Athenian idols but the very practice of idolatry itself. Statues of wood and stone, he observed, were only that—statues of wood and stone.

The apostle concluded his presentation with a discussion about two concepts that make moral relativists cringe still today—repentance and resurrection. Most of Paul's listeners choked at the possibility of an after-life and the day of reckoning that belief implies. Most of Paul's listeners refused to believe because they did not want to repent. A few signed on with Paul to learn more. Most folded their arms across their robes and turned their attention to the next new idea that came mincing and prancing across the stage of the Areopagus.

Paul respected the intellectuals to whom he spoke. Even so, he did not accept their ideas. We do well in our contacts with those outside the faith if we maintain that distinction. We can respect the people without approving of their practices. We can respect the people without twisting our own theology into a pretzel of relativism.

Well-meaning couples who decide their daughter will attend worship one week with her Christian parent and the next week with her Jewish or Islamic parent create all kinds of confusion in their child's mind and heart.

Well-meaning couples who let their 6- or 8- or 12-year-old son decide when, where, and how to worship create all kinds of questions and doubts in that boy's mind.

Well-meaning couples who explain away genuine spiritual differences between themselves by telling their children they have simply "agreed to disagree" plant the seeds of spiritual relativism in their children's hearts.

None of the child-rearing questions you may face will voluntarily hop in the cauldron on your kitchen stove and beg to be boiled down to an easy resolution. But the alternative to respectful family discussion is fear, confusion, and frustration for every member of the family, especially the children.

Christian parents must choose their words prayerfully so that disagreement does not degenerate into an excuse to teach disrespect. Non-Christian parents married to Christians must also choose their words and actions with care so as not to ridicule or undercut the faith that the Christian parent is trying to pass on to the child(ren).

Both parents need to:

- Respect one another's beliefs.

- Communicate with one another—clearly and honestly—when those beliefs or practices cause conflict.

- Demonstrate the difference between respect and approval in the way they treat one another before, during, and after they disagree.

Will My Children Have Faith?

No doubt the most tender spot in a Christian parent's heart lies just beneath the surface of this question. When Jesus and His love mean everything to us, we quite naturally want to do whatever we can to make sure our children know that love too and that they will carry the assurance of the Savior's love and forgiveness with them into adulthood.

God's command to remember the Sabbath should be enough to encourage regular attendance at public worship services. But let me quote a recent study that provides striking support for the practical outcome of obeying the Third Commandment. These particular researchers found that:

- 6% of the children who had grown up in a home where neither parent worshiped regularly became regular attenders in adulthood.

- 15% of those children who had grown up in a home where Mom took the kids to church regularly became regular attenders in adulthood.

- 55% of those children who had grown up in a home where Dad took the kids to church regularly became regular attenders in adulthood.

- 73% of those children who had grown up in a home where both parents regularly worshiped with their children regularly became regular attenders in adulthood.

Good worship attendance habits and the modeling that parents do *does* make a difference in children's lives.

Statistics like these can frighten Christian parents who live in spiritually mixed marriages. Still, church attendance is only one of several factors that help shape a child's future spiritual direction.

Another study has noted that a single conversation in which a parent expressed his or her faith in the Savior's love had more impact on a child's future spiritual maturity than sending that child to church for an entire year! More impact than an entire year of church attendance!

Now, of course, Christian parents will want to do both. They will want to worship with their children, and they will also want to talk often with their children about our Savior and the difference He makes in our lives.

Still, if your family cannot or does not attend church together, you need not lose heart. If you've failed in your witness to your children in the past, you need not give up hope. God forgives. He forgives even sins of neglect, even sins that hurt others in our family.

God's Spirit has promised to be at work as you speak His Word and as you live out the faith in deeds that validate your words. You are not responsible for saving your family. They already have a Savior. You dare not take His saving work onto your own shoulders.

Instead, your job is to keep on planting the seed of God's Word, to keep on showing Jesus' love, to keep on relying on Him to hold you and your children close to Himself, and to keep on praying for your children and your spouse.

If you have not done so lately or if you've never done so at all, take a minute or two right now to turn the responsibility for your children's spiritual well-being over to the only one who can make the seed of the Word sprout and grow—your great God. Then rest in His love for you and your family. Rest in His forgiveness for your failures to be a perfect witness to your spouse and family. Rest in His compassion and care for all the members of your family, for *all* the members of your family—even you.

Before You Go On

1. What differences in viewpoint are (or do you anticipate will be) the greatest points of conflict and concern for you and your spouse as your

children grow?

a. Which of these are truly spiritual issues?

b. Which of them might be simply differences of opinion and temperament?

c. How might each of these differences best be addressed?

2. Why do you think a parent's personal comments about the importance of the Lord Jesus and His love for us makes such a powerful impact in the hearts of his/her children? What implications do you see in this for your relationship with your own child(ren)?

3. What parts of this chapter rang especially true for you? Explain.

4. What parts of this chapter gave you hope? Explain.

7

WHAT ABOUT MY CHURCH?

Our society has elevated the pioneer spirit to a godlike status. We Christians find ourselves bowing down to worship this idol perhaps not much less often than the unbelievers around us. We kneel at its feet every time we grit our teeth over an impossible situation and declare, "I can do this myself!" We grovel before this idol every time we think about someone else's problems and ask ourselves, "Why can't (s)he get it together?"

Believers who live in spiritually mixed marriages perhaps see most clearly some of the ways this supposed "tough-minded independence" has made inroads in the church. Christ has left His church in the world, and we, sad to say, have incorporated much of the world's thinking into the church. If Sabine Baring-Gould were to write "Onward, Christian Soldiers" today, the lyrics might go something like this:

> Like a fallen army,
> Moans the church of God.

Brothers, we are lying
Where our fathers trod.
We are so divided;
Shattered body we.
Lord, please clear our vision,
Make us family!

The kind of spiritual loneliness described in chapter 2 finds its only cure in Christian community. But who's responsible for seeing to it that you and I find the support we need from our brothers and sisters in Christ?

If all of us lived in a sinless world and if we attended a perfect church, our quest for support would end in the middle of a highway—half-way between our home and that of our Christian brothers and sisters. The believers who know you would understand your situation with perfect clarity. They would reach out at once in every time of trouble to provide exactly the support you needed.

You, on your part, would receive that help gladly and unashamed of your need for it. You would accept it as an indication of your Savior's love for you, and you would see your fellow believers as channels of divine love into your life. You would continue to express your needs and count on God to meet those needs through the people in His church, your local congregation.

Few of God's children belong to a given congregation more than five minutes before they realize that we do not live in a sinless world and no one has yet founded a perfect Christian congregation. Maybe even as you read the description above, you found yourself shaking your head in discouragement, remembering one or more example of insensitivity shown you by your church family.

On the other hand, maybe you find yourself nodding in the sad agreement of confession, recognizing that you haven't always dropped your pride long enough to express your pain or to ask for specific kinds of help. Maybe you've asked once or twice and then given up in despair, believing no one really cares or wants to help.

Don't Give Up on God

A public service announcement written specifically for children who find themselves in danger or distress includes a song that goes like this:

> *Tell your mom, tell your dad*
> *If you're scared or hurt or sad.*
> *Keep on telling 'til somebody says,*
> *"I'm going to help you—now!"*

If you're hurt, if you're scared, or sad, or spiritually lonely, keep on telling. Don't give up. Don't give in to Satan's lie that you can do it by yourself. You can't. Your soul will shrivel and die. Your heavenly Father made you for a much higher purpose. Your

Savior has promised you the kind of abundant life you've always dreamed about. Don't settle for less.

Look for safe people in your congregation who will listen to your needs. If you're not sure whom to trust, ask your pastor for suggestions. Perhaps he might even be willing to take the initiative in getting the two of you together the first time.

If you meet with continual rebuffs even after you've made repeated, polite attempts to reach out, you may need to think and pray about finding a new church home. I hesitate to suggest this because of the dangers involved in giving up too soon and because of the terrible pain such a decision can bring. It takes tremendous courage to begin again, but for your own eternal good and for the good of your family, you may—in certain cases—need to take that step.

Let's discuss the steps involved in that first. As you will see, the process is a drastic one. It's a process to be used only in the most extreme cases. Once we've looked at what's involved in carrying out such a decision, we'll go back and look at some alternatives. Alternatives that will, in most cases, seem at that point preferable to divorcing your congregation.

In the event you decide that the situation in your present congregation has become so damaging to you that you and your family must leave, make an appointment with your pastor. Politely but firmly state your decision and the reasoning on which you based it. Ask him to suggest a congregation that can offer the kind of support and teaching you and your family need.

I know this kind of encounter sounds risky. I know it will seem easier simply to disappear over the horizon. But remember that your Lord may want one last chance to bring about reconciliation. No matter how impossible that may seem, you need to give the Holy Spirit a chance to help you and your congregation or pastor understand one another. Even if you decide you still must leave, at least you can leave without bitterness.

Also remember that you need not reenact World War II. You need not turn your conversation into a firestorm of accusations. You need not hurl recriminations, listing every hurt or insult you think you've received.

To avoid that possibility, ask the Lord to keep these guidelines in the forefront of your consciousness as you talk:

- Keep your goal in mind—finding the kind of spiritual support that will see you through a time of longterm personal challenge. You and your family need support. Your goal is not to hurt someone else, but to get help for yourself.

- Keep your focus on problem-solving, not on blaming or accusing anyone else. You are looking for a congregation that is open to ministering to someone in your situation and that will invite you to serve others in appropriate ways too.

- Keep your conversation as positive as possible; express genuine thankfulness for any help and concern that you have received. Admit any sins you've committed that have kept the kettle of discontent simmering and ask for forgiveness.

- Keep your heart and mind open to hear what the Lord might want you to learn about yourself and about more effective ways to ask for help in the future.

Before It Gets to That Point ...

Take it from someone who once left a congregation out of frustration and anger, it's not spiritually healthful. It's not physically or emotionally healthful either. If you picture the process as a real, though invisible amputation, you would not miss the mark by much.

Sometimes bailing out may prove to be the most loving, godly thing you can do. Still, on the authority of the Scriptures and on the basis of my own experience, I advise you to make sure your engine is in flames, you are headed toward the face of a mountain, and you have lost control of the plane before you decide to ditch. Leaving will prove painful no matter what. I can almost guarantee it.

And if it does not, you need to look at the reasons you committed yourself to that particular church-family in the first place. You need to examine the motives that lay behind the work you did and the money you donated there. You need to think about the kind of ties you allowed yourself to form with the other believers there and the kinds of relationships you avoided.

You need to look at these things not to beat yourself up, but to prevent yourself from making the same mistakes again in your new church home. You see, if you place all the blame on others, you are almost certainly setting yourself up for the very same feelings of rejection and spiritual isolation you are trying to escape.

So, before you decide to divorce your congregation and fire your pastor, try some less drastic measures first. Measures such as these:

- Pray for your congregation and its leadership. Not just for a day or a week, but for several months or even years. Pray, too, for your fellow believers there and for yourself and your family.

- Ask God to give you the courage you need to keep on asking for appropriate kinds of help. Also ask Him to supply the energy you need to reach out in love to others who find themselves in your situation. Keep on asking for these things.

- Look back at the suggestions in chapter 2 (pp. 30–31). Pray about which of these the Lord may want you to try (or try again). Then do it.

- Talk with your congregation's evangelism chairperson. Express specific concerns, especially about your spouse and/or children. Share the "Suggestions for Congregations" from the section below. Ask which of these may already be a part of your congregation's ministry. Volunteer to help put some of the others into practice.

In general, rely on God's grace to enable you to find or create ways to be part of the solution, not just a victim of your circumstances. God may want to use you as the answer to someone else's prayers. He may even want to use you as part of the answer to your own!

Suggestions for Congregations—the ABCs

A is for attitude. All ministry begins here. Ask yourselves questions such as these:

- Do we see our members' unbelieving spouses as enemies, as the "bad guys"? Or do we see them as individuals for whom Jesus Christ bled and died, as potential brothers and sisters in the faith?

- Do we see our members' unchurched partners as targets for our evangelism adventures, as potential notches in the binding of our Bibles? Or do we see them as eternal souls who will, by definition, live forever—either with us in the kingdom of our Father or shut away from His love in eternal darkness?

- When unbelievers attend congregational events with their spouses, do we ignore them? greet them? help them feel at ease?

We can treat unbelievers with respect. We can treat them as fellow human beings. Agnosticism is not a contagious disease. Those who don't know Christ do not have two heads. Most of them are not ax murderers. We can relax and be ourselves. We can talk about baseball and about the new taco hut down the street. We need not—and we should not—try to make a pious impression. It's probably the surest way to confirm the ridiculous caricature of Christians so common on late night TV.

An attitude of concern for the member spouse is critical too. Look for ways to support those who are alone on Sunday because their spouse does not join them in worship.

Some may jump at the chance to join a support group if the congregation's leaders will set one up and input minimal energy to keep it running. (This book could provide discussion material as the group gets started.) Other members might treasure a well-thought-out referral to another individual person in similar family circumstances, the idea being that the two will agree to offer one another mutual encouragement. Still other members might be eternally grateful for counseling, for help in sorting out one or more aspects of their lives.

In short, look for ways to help believing spouses bear their family burdens. This will in turn enable them to be better witnesses at home as our Lord intends (1 Peter 3:1ff.).

B is for bowling. Yes, bowling. Congregations serious about ministry to members' unchurched spouses will do well to think of ways to show an interest in the humanity we share with those we would like to reach:

- Set up friendship evangelism events without labeling them as that (e.g., ice-cream socials after VBS closing services, softball teams for adults or kids, free Easter breakfasts). Provide opportunities for nonmembers to get to know their spouses' church friends in a relaxed, no-pressure atmosphere. Affirm their participation (e.g., "How great of you to give up your morning to be here with us and your family!"). Then intentionally use the events to make new contacts and enhance established relationships with unchurched spouses.

- Show concern for the well-being of families by refusing to allow even willing members (perhaps especially willing members!) to overcommit themselves to the activities of your congregation. Too many Christians try to live at church as if they had no family. Too many churches let it happen. An unchurched wife will soon come to resent the congregation that absorbs 98% of her husband's free time. An unbelieving husband will soon come to resent the God who seems to demand most of his wife's energy. Help all members strike a God-pleasing balance between commitment to family and to congregation.

- Support marriage and the family. But don't make them an idol. We worship Christ, not marriage. Counseling someone to stay in a physically abusive home is irresponsible, even in the name of "godly submission." So is counseling someone to stay in an alcoholic home, in a verbally abusive environment, or in a situation that is otherwise dangerous. Help the person being abused find a refuge from the abuse, help that person find competent psychological and spiritual counseling, and then—and only then—see if the marriage can be saved.

C is for crisis. Visit families during times of crisis. Offer the kind of help you can give. Keep in mind that a crisis is not by definition always a negative event. The birth of a child, the first day on a new job, a move into a new home can all be crisis points too. Positive crises.

Also remember that some believers will not send up flares and shoot off rockets when they find themselves in crisis. We need to listen and watch for quieter signals.

- If Lucy begins to miss two or three out of every four worship services, someone needs to ask some gentle questions about what's going on in her life. Maybe Larry has forbidden her to attend church. Maybe she's become discouraged in her struggle to get the kids up and ready for Sunday school. People often say as much by their absence as by their presence.

- If Cynthia mentions the death of Craig's father, visit Cynthia and Craig. You need not stay an hour. You need not preach a sermon. Simply express your concern. (E.g., "Death—any death— is a terrible thing. It hurts a lot. I don't want to push, but if you need to talk, I'd like to listen— anytime.")

- If David asks you to pray for Debbie, who's pregnant with their second child, pray. And write Debbie a note congratulating her and telling her of your prayers.

- If Robert mentions that Rachael will be graduated from the university and is looking for a job, drop by with a graduation cupcake, a card, and an offer to make a job contact or two for her.

Ministry to and with spiritually mixed families—it's as simple as ABC. But as complicated as Kierkegaard too. Unless a congregation approaches this ministry intentionally, chances are that it simply will fall by the wayside. Pray and think about what our Lord might have you do in your particular congregation.

Before You Go On

1. How could you support your congregation's ministry to unchurched spouses? Which of these ideas do you think the Lord might want you to try? Why? When will you do that?

2. As you read this chapter, did you become aware of any unspoken needs in your own life that you could ask someone in your congregation to help you meet? To whom could you talk about that? When will you do that?

3. What has your congregation or your pastor done or said that you found helpful and supportive? How did you (will you) express your thanks?

❧ Appendix A—
Before You Leap ...

One autumn a friend and I took a 10-mile hike through a dense forest. You can picture it, can't you? The air crisp and fragrant. A sapphire sky. The crunch, crunch, crunch as we walked through the leaves. Those leaves still unfallen dancing golden, fire-red, and fading emerald in the breeze around us. Our language has no adjectives adequate for such a day. We walked for hours, savoring each minute.

The joy ended abruptly for me early that evening. I began to itch. This was no minor skin irritation. An hour later, my legs begged me to find a hospital that would administer total anesthesia.

I ignored the proverb about those who medicate themselves having foolish patients. I knew beyond a doubt that chiggers had burrowed themselves beneath my skin and were at that very moment plotting ways to drive me to insanity. Frantic for relief, I bought out all the bottles of chigger glop I could find at the closest convenience store.

Two days later, I still couldn't sit still. Those chiggers were taking a long time to surrender. I showed photos from the hike to one of the editorial assistants in my office that *morning, partly to share the fun Linda and I had had and partly to turn my attention away from the infernal itching.*

When Phoebe came to one of the photos in the middle of the stack, she gasped. She stared at me, eyebrows raised. Silence. Finally she spoke. "Why are you sitting in poison oak?" she asked.

The answer to that was simple. I hadn't known— until that moment—what poison oak looked like. I showed the parallel photo a few minutes later to Linda who worked in the same building. As she stared at it, I asked her Phoebe's question, "Why are you sitting in poison oak?"

Her answer was simple too. She hadn't noticed. The spectacular view. The nearby creek with its rustic wooden footbridge. The urge to capture all the beauty around us on film. All of these had conspired to divert her attention from something that in the end mattered more. (No pun intended.)

As I smoothed on calamine lotion later that day, several antihistamine tablets later, I studied the photograph of myself with the intensity of desperation. Never would I tangle with poison oak again. Not if I could help it!

I had only one excuse for such a ridiculous mistake. Growing up on the Iowa prairie, I had never developed an interest in forest flora. After all, how important could it be?

It May Not Seem Important Now ...

Perhaps as you read this, you are contemplating a lifelong marriage partnership with someone who does not share your Christian faith. Maybe you've already committed yourself to a partnership like that by getting engaged.

You might not phrase the question quite so bluntly as I will, but you may find yourself asking, "How important can it be? How critical a difference can my faith make in our relationship?"

Or maybe you haven't stopped to ask questions at all. Maybe the swirl of wedding plans, of finding a home to share, of romance, and of passion have diverted your attention away from something that will, in reality, matter much more.

If so, I plead with you—as maybe others who care about you have in recent weeks and months—don't let the current of activities sweep you into the river of reality unaware. Don't make a decision as important as marriage by default. Examine the evidence and ask your Savior to clear your mind so that the conclusions you reach will anchor themselves in bedrock far deeper than the emotions of the moment.

It would be foolish of you to base your conclusion on my opinions. I've never met you, and I've never had to make the decision facing you. I've never hiked that forest. If you plan to settle down in that particular woods, though, you need to do some exploring before you start to construct your cabin. Here are some ways to do that.

- Study some Scriptures that apply specifically to your decision. You might begin with 1 Cor. 7:39

or 2 Cor. 6:14–18 and the verses that surround each of these texts. Write out for yourself what these passages seem to mean as you think about them and as you pray for the Holy Spirit's guidance.

- Ask your pastor to loan you a commentary or two. Compare what the writers say about the verses you've studied with what you have written. Again, ask for the Holy Spirit's guidance as you search His Word. Ask Him to show you His heart of love toward you.

- Talk over your situation and the Scriptures you've studied with a mature believer whom you trust. Better still, talk with several. Your pastor. One of your congregation's elders or deacons. A Sunday school teacher whom you respect. Ask for their counsel. Tell them you're not looking simply for a yes/no verdict, but that you're especially interested in the reasons behind their opinion and the way their reasoning fits in with that of the Scriptures.

- Interview two or more Christians who have been married to unbelieving partners for a while—ideally, five years or longer. Ask about the problems they've faced. Ask about their spiritual well-being. Ask about challenges with their children. Ask how they've addressed these challenges. Get their advice. (If you don't know whom to ask, your pastor may be willing to suggest names. If you're too shy to call, your pastor may even be willing to ask one or more of these people to call you.)

No Surprises

In an earlier chapter, readers of this book met Lucy and Larry. (You may want to read their story on pp. 11–12.) Lucy made several deadly assumptions before her wedding day. She assumed that her love for Larry and his love for her would always burn hot enough and bright enough to vaporize any problems that could arise in their relationship. She assumed that the marriage would change Larry or that she herself could change him after the wedding. She assumed that when Larry became a husband and certainly when he became a father, he would realize his need for the Lord and his responsibility to exercise spiritual leadership in his family.

Unfortunately, Lucy's assumptions evaporated into thin air shortly after the two returned from their honeymoon.

Lucy didn't want to talk to Larry about spiritual things before the wedding ceremony because she feared a conversation like that might drive him away. She didn't want to offend him. She didn't want him to think of her as some kind of fanatic. So she said nothing about the one thing that she would later consider the most important thing in her life.

It doesn't take a rocket scientist to figure out that Lucy didn't trust Larry very much. From all outward appearances, she also had some serious misgivings about the strength of their relationship. If one or two conversations about Jesus Christ and His cross would derail their wedding plans, one must wonder how long that train would have stayed on the tracks in any case.

Assumptions about another person's beliefs and commitments seldom prove very accurate. You cannot rely on what you think the one you love might believe or want to practice in his or her relationship with you or with the Lord. Ask. Talk. Keep on talking.

People who buy a new house usually have one iron-clad demand—no surprises. Bosses who interview and hire a new employee usually have one iron-clad rule—no surprises. Supervisors on an assembly line, directors in charge of Broadway plays, teachers responsible for fourth-grade classes usually have one goal carved in stone—no surprises.

A home owner, a supervisor, a teacher, a director—all can handle many challenges, even huge challenges, if they know what they're up against. People who work together to make money live and die by the no-surprise rule. How much more important then should this rule be to people who intend to work together to make a life?

If you're convinced at this point that you need to talk with your potential partner about your spiritual values and your Christian faith, the talk sheet on pp. 138–144 might help you get started. If you're still not convinced that you need to ask for that conversation, reread this section. Then interview some people who have lived a few years in a marriage that began like Larry and Lucy's. Talk to the Lord and to someone you trust about why you're avoiding discussions about your faith. It's critical.

Put Away the Shotgun

A friend of mine served as pastor in a small parish in rural Iowa. Just out of the seminary, he eagerly awaited his first wedding. He took nearly 20 couples through a thorough premarital counseling program during the first three years of his ministry. And in those years, he performed not one wedding ceremony. Virtually every couple he counseled backed out at some point along the line.

The first four or five times it happened, his friends commiserated with him. The next four or five times, they teased him a bit. By the 16th couple, the heckling grew unmerciful.

At the end of his third year, my friend finally officiated at his first wedding. It was a toss-up as to whether he or the couple felt happier that day.

Joking aside, this young pastor's thorough approach probably caused some pain. Yet he undoubtedly prevented a good deal more pain in more than three dozen lives. He helped the people he counseled to see that even when good reasons exist to marry, sometimes there are also good reasons not to—at least, reasons not to marry just yet. Let's close with three stories to illustrate.

Vicki has dated Morgan for two years. She knows and loves Jesus and she worships Him weekly. Morgan admits he's an agnostic. It's okay for Vicki to be a Christian and maybe for most women he believes. But men, being less emotional, are above that need. At least, he is.

Vicki found out a week ago that she's pregnant. Morgan wants to marry her. Vicki is afraid of what her parents will do if she turns Morgan down. But more than that, Vicki feels guilty for having had intercourse with Morgan repeatedly over the past several months.

"How can I tell him I won't marry him because he's not a Christian when I haven't lived up to my own moral standards?" Vicki asks herself.

Vicki is about to walk down the aisle, motivated not by commitment to Morgan and to Christ's will for her life, but motivated by fear and guilt.

Can you see both the emotional power and the terrible lack of logic in Vicki's question? There's a simpler solution for Vicki. Not an easy solution, but a much cleaner, more healthy one.

Jesus forgives. Vicki needs to let Him do that. She may need to ask someone trustworthy to assure her of that, to absolve her of her sins, and to pray with her for the courage to make a wise decision about whether to keep her baby or to give it up for adoption.

Her present course will carry her into the deep waters of despair—and quickly. Our Lord wants us to know and believe His forgiveness. That forgiveness can keep us from compounding our grief. We need not try to cover up our sins by committing more of them. We need not wrestle one mistake into submission by making two more.

Knowing Christ's total forgiveness, we can do all things through Him, for He provides the strength we need (cf. Phil. 4:13). A platform of fear and guilt will never serve as a strong foundation on which to build a marriage.

Eric's family razzes him without end about his single lifestyle. Eric will turn 34 on his next birthday. He dates regularly. In fact, his relationships often last three, four, or five months. Still, Eric hasn't found the woman to whom he wants to commit his love for life.

Usually, Eric takes the kidding good-naturedly. But in the past several months he finds himself wondering, worrying really, about whether or not he'll ever marry.

"Maybe I am too picky, just like my dad says," Eric finds himself thinking. "Maybe I will wind up alone in old age, just like Mom says."

Eric has been seeing Stephanie for two months. He's dated her before—last year for five months. She's lukewarm about her faith, though she does attend church with Eric when he asks her. Eric feels comfortable with her. They laugh a lot when they're together. They communicate openly about their feelings, about their likes and dislikes.

Eric likes Stephanie. He may even love her. She has already told him of her love for him. Whenever they're together, it seems that Eric fights an ongoing, 18-round battle with sexual temptation. Despite all that, though, Stephanie's coolness toward Christ troubles Eric.

Can you empathize with the pressure Eric feels, both from those around him and from inside himself? How easily Eric could give in to the pressure. How easily he could make decisions based on the fear no one else will ever come along for him and he'll be left alone. Permanently. And frankly, how easy it would be to make decisions based on his very real desire to jump into bed with Stephanie.

Eric and Stephanie may end up at the altar. Or they may not. But before Eric stands there with Stephanie, he needs to have some serious conversations with her about her faith and about what Jesus Christ means in his life. Eric also needs to ask his family to put the teasing on hold. Politely, but firmly, and with as much or as little explanation as he wants to give, Eric must ask them to back off. If they do not, he may need to limit contact with them.

Knowing Christ's total love for us and His commitment to bring about His best for our lives, we can wait for Him to do that. We need not let ourselves be stampeded into something that will almost surely turn out to be less than His best. A platform of desperation and loneliness will never serve as a strong foundation on which to build a marriage.

Della grew up in an abusive home. Her father berated her seemingly at every turn. Several times a month he would hit her. Now 19, Della still lives at home so she can afford to attend classes at the local community college. She dreams of becoming an architect someday. She's smart enough and creative enough to do it. But she's not so sure of that. And, true to form, Dad reinforces her doubts whenever he gets a chance.

Della knows that her Lord has helped her through what just about anyone would consider a terrible adolescence. Jesus is important to her. But so is David.

Della met David in her college calculus class. It was very nearly the legendary love-at-first sight syndrome. The two are inseparable. David has begged Della to move in with him, but she has stood firm in her desire to obey God. So now, David begs her to marry him.

More than anything else, Della would like to get out from under her family's roof. How lovely coming home at night could be if she knew she didn't face the prospect of a continuous screaming match until bed time.

Della worries about David's belief in reincarnation and his theory that "all religions lead to the same God." Still, whenever Della's dad and mom crank up the decibel level on still another argument, Della wonders how important David's unorthodox theories really are.

Can you identify with Della's need to find an escape hatch? Or to create one by the sheer force of her will? Can anyone blame her for looking a second, a third, and even a fourth time at David's proposal?

Still, Della needs to think longterm—for her own good as well as for David's. Maybe some conversations with David will help him straighten out his thinking. Maybe some research on Della's part will reveal community or congregational resources that can get her out of her parents' house on a semipermanent (until graduation) basis so that she can think more rationally about David's offer.

Della probably needs to work through many relationship issues with a wise counselor before she considers entering any relationship as permanent as God intends marriage to be. Her pastor should be able to point her toward the kind of help she needs. In any case, she dare not see David as her savior. The last thing she needs is to begin a family of her own that will repeat her childhood family history.

Anyone who understands human behavior will

verify the fact that a person who, for one reason or another, lacks a strong personal identity, confidence, and contentment before marriage will not magically find those things in marriage. Marriage can deepen contentment, can deepen intimacy, can deepen identity and integrity, but it cannot create those things.

Knowing Christ's great compassion for you and His promises to make a way for you to escape the temptations of this life, you can avoid the dangers that come with trying to blow your own escape hatch in the fuselage of your circumstances. For you, as for Della, a platform of desperation and self-contempt will never serve as a strong foundation for marriage.

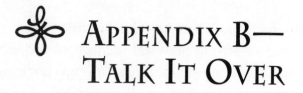

Appendix B—
Talk It Over

Directions: Think through these questions on your own at first. Then get together with your partner to discuss your answers. Take turns reading the questions and answering them.

Listen carefully to what the other person says. Pay attention to the feelings his/her words evoke in you.

Take your time. You may spend an entire evening on one question. That's okay. Simply go on to the next question the next time you sit down together. Your goal is not to answer all the questions in the shortest time possible; your goal is to understand one another's beliefs, values, and behaviors.

God

1. Pretend you're 80 years old and have become famous. A writer interviews you in preparation for writing your biography. What would you tell the writer about your early spiritual beliefs and experiences?

2. I think God is_____ (*fill in the blank*)
   because _____ (*fill*

in the blank). Now go back and answer this question five more times.

3. What do you think of Jesus Christ? What impact does He have on your life?

Worship Life

4. For me, the Bible is ... (*circle one*)

   a. a big book my grandma used to read.

   b. the Word of God.

   c. a collection of interesting stories and old letters.

   d. a love letter from Jesus' heart to mine.

   e. a book I tried to read once, but got confused and gave up.

   f. the product of a much-less developed culture than our own.

   g. a rule book for right living.

   h. _____

5. Rate the importance of each of these things in your life on a scale from 0–10, 0 meaning "not important in the least" and 10 meaning "the most important thing in my life."

   ___ knowing Jesus
   ___ attending church
   ___ belonging to a church

___ having time to pray each day
___ reading the Bible
___ my Baptism
___ attending Holy Communion
___ serving other people in practical ways
___ giving money to meet other people's needs
___ spending time with people who share my beliefs and values

6. If my spouse wants to practice his/her faith after we're married, I will ... (*check one*)

___ oppose it.
___ tolerate it.
___ respect him/her for it.
___ gently help him/her break away from it.
___ do whatever it takes to make that possible.
___ join him/her in the outward rituals (e.g., worship attendance).
___ open myself as wide as possible to understand and accept for myself what he/she believes, even though I don't now.

(*Now go back and answer these questions the way you think your partner will. When you compare answers, how satisfied do you feel with your partner's answers?*)

Church Involvement

(The partner who goes to church most often should answer the next four questions.)

7. How do you think you will feel getting up and

going to worship services alone? Will this affect how often you attend? Why or why not?

8. Suppose your partner never goes with you—not even at special times such as Christmas and Easter. How do you think you'll react? How do you think it will affect your relationship with him/her?

9. You share the most intimate part of yourself (your relationship with Jesus and your service to Him) with friends at church. At this point, does your partner share that spiritual intimacy with you too? If not, how will that affect your relationship with him/her? with Jesus?

10. How would you like your partner to treat your pastor? your Christian friends? How will you show respect for your partner's friends? What does "respect" mean to you in these specific sets of relationships?

(*The partner who does not attend church or who attends only occasionally should answer the next four questions.*)

11. How will you feel if your partner gets up Sunday mornings to go to church and leaves you alone? How do you think this will affect your relationship? Explain.

12. How do you feel about going along with your

partner to a worship service on special holidays such as Christmas and Easter? How do you think the pattern you develop will affect your relationship with your partner? Explain.

13. Your partner shares a very deep, very important part of himself/herself with friends at church. How do you feel about not sharing that—not because of a deliberate decision your partner makes but by virtue of the circumstances? How do you think it will affect your relationship with him/her? Explain.

14. Will you respect your partner's pastor? your partner's Christian friends? What does "respect" mean to you in this specific instance?

The Children

15. Are our spiritual differences big enough to be a factor in our decision whether or not to have children? Explain.

16. If we have children, in what faith will we raise them? Why?

17. Will each of us agree to support the spiritual training the children receive? How far is each of us willing to go in that support?

    (*Check all that apply.*)

    ___ speaking and acting with respect toward one

another's beliefs

___ getting the kids up and dressed for worship

___ sending them to church and Sunday school

___ going with them to church and Sunday school

___ praying meal prayers as a family (letting the children do so)

___ teaching bedtime prayers to the children (letting them pray bedtime prayers)

___ sending them to a Christian school

___ paying tuition so they can attend a Christian school

___ attending services and programs in which the children participate (e.g., Christmas services, church picnics)

Family Finances

18. What part of our income will go to support my church (my partner's church)? How will we review this decision if either of us wants to change it?

19. Will we support other programs with our financial resources (e.g., foreign missionaries, community charities, Christian colleges)? How will we decide?

Last, But Not Least

20. When I die, I will _____

    _____

    _____

    I think/believe/know this because

    _____

    _____

21. When I hear my partner's answer to this question, I feel _____

    _____

    _____

    because _____

    _____

    _____